Listen! Songs and Poems of Canada

"I shout Love . . . Love . . . It's a net
scooping us weltering, fighting for joy
hearts beating out new tempos against each other!"

Milton Acorn

Listen!

Songs and Poems
of Canada

Edited by

Homer Hogan
Associate Professor of English
University of Guelph

Assistant Editor

Dorothy Hogan
Bishop Macdonell High School

Methuen Canadian Literature Series
Methuen
Toronto   London   Sydney   Wellington

Library of Congress Catalogue Card Number 72-76594
ISBN   pb   0   458   90900   9
       hc   0   458   90940   8

Designed by Carl Brett.
Printed and bound in Canada.

76 75   3 4 5 6

Photo credits:

Stan Rosenthall, ii; Early Morning Productions Limited, x;
"Bow Lake, Alberta," by Byron Harmon, one of Canada's
greatest photographers, courtesy of Don Harmon, 5;
AM Records, 18; *Toronto Star*, 24, 30, 43, 95; Peter
Wilkinson 38, 80, 119, 140; RCA, 48; Boot Records, 60;
GRT Records 66, 74; Ernst Haas, 78; Dorothy Hogan,
88, 111, 149; Canadian Composer, 90; Warner Brothers,
104; Capitol Records, 122; Paul Newberry, 128, 133, 157;
Reprise Records, 130.

Contents

Introduction

During the past few years, my wife and I have been asking young people all over Canada to tell us the Canadian songs and poems that really speak to them. The result is this book.

But a few warnings are in order. First the readers should know that *Listen!* does not pretend to represent the best-known songs and poems of young Canada. We did not use questionnaires. We simply talked with many individual students, young workers and young writers and asked them what they had discovered that seemed worth keeping for contemplation and enjoyment. Consequently, there are many works here the reader may never have seen before—poems by French-Canadians, Indians, Eskimos, high school students, and writers like Red Lane, bill bissell, Dale Zieroth, Kenneth Yukich, Marc Plourde, Ken Belford, Lloyd Abbey, and Peter Trower who are just beginning to gain the attention they deserve.

Many readers will even be surprised by the songs, not so much because they have not heard them, but because they have never realized the scope and significance of contemporary Canadian song literature. Ritchie York, in *Axes, Chops, and Hot Licks* (Edmonton: M. G. Hurtig Ltd., 1971), thoroughly documents the long suppression of Canadian popular music by Canadian radio stations. The success of Canadian performers in the United States and the action of the federal government to encourage Canadian music on radio, were events which finally allowed us to hear what our musicians were achieving. But there is still little being done to distinguish the Canadian music we hear from that of American and British performers. *Listen!* attempts to encourage that distinction, not only to strengthen our national awareness, but also to make evident a distinctive Canadian style of song poetry whose rich possibilities of development need nurture and appreciation.

In addition to works by young Canadians, *Listen!* also includes poems by older Canadian poets. The reason is that *Listen!* is intended to present poetry that young people may discover genuinely *belongs* to them, since it helps them to answer their main questions in life: Who am I? Where do I come from? Where am I going? What can I do? My students often find such insights in the works of long established Canadian poets as well as in the poems of their contemporaries. *Listen!* therefore tries to include enough of our older poetry to provide a sense of the living poetic heritage which the young are carrying on.

Previously unpublished works printed in *Listen!* include Irving Layton's recent poem, "Xmas Eve", and the poetry of 24 students from secondary schools throughout Canada. The student poems result from a call for poetry that I sent out to high schools from coast to coast. Over 6,000 young people replied with about 13,000 submissions, probably the greatest outpouring of youth and poetry in Canadian history. The poems I selected were chosen not only for their quality, but also for their ability to voice feelings of individual young people about the themes developed in the various groupings of songs and poems. Each voice is unique, and considered together the poems reveal how richly varied are the gifts and responses of Canadian youth. My selection, of course, can convey only a hint of the treasure which Canada's high school students have presented me. Now I am preparing a supplement to *Listen!* devoted entirely to these riches, one which I hope will do further justice to the talents of our young people.

The connections between the songs and poems will be self-evident after the discussion of the songs for each section. Each song introduces a theme or mood which the poems that follow then explore. Song poetry is generally simpler than spoken poetry and so provides a natural beginning point for those who want to follow the magic ways of words. It is essential, however, to hear the music behind each song poem if the lyrics are to be a true beginning of poetic exploration.*

My deepest gratitude is extended to the hundreds of teachers and thousands of students who answered my call for poetry with such generosity and enthusiasm. I also want to thank the countless other young people whose recommendations of songs and poems formed the basis of this book. Nor can I underestimate the contributions of Radio Gryphon at the University of Guelph; Operations Co-ordinator Ian McDiarmid and his staff spent many hours—with the kind support of Station Manager James Manning—in assembling for us a splendid collection of Canadian popular music. Paul Parry, Lucille Hanlon, and Louise Edwards of the University of Guelph library also were extremely helpful. And I must offer special thanks to certain unsung heroes whose long and successful struggles on behalf of Canadian song made Listen! possible: Estelle Klein, Festival Director of the annual Mariposa Folk Festival at Toronto Islands; Richard Flohill, editor of Canadian Composer (CAPAC); Bernie Fiedler of Toronto's Riverboat; Bernie Finkelstein of True North Records; Walt Grealis, editor of RPM; and rock columnist, Ritchie York—to mention only a few of the most outstanding.

*For a fuller discussion of the relations between song and "pure" poetry, see Homer Hogan, Poetry of Relevance, Vols. 1 and 2 (Agincourt, Ont.: Methuen, 1970), esp. pp. 16-20, 23-26 in Vol. 1, and pp. 13-14, 19-22 in Vol. 2.)

Gordon Lightfoot

1

Those who say that Gordon Lightfoot is the founder of contemporary Canadian song can make a pretty convincing case. Throughout the renaissance of song poetry during the sixties, Lightfoot was not only Canada's leading troubadour, but also had more songs recorded by North American performers than anyone except Bob Dylan. What makes Lightfoot synonymous with Canadian song, however, is more than his outstanding gifts as a singer-composer. The fact is that Lightfoot crystallized in his songs, personality, and singing style the most striking features of the English-Canadian "identity". Admittedly, that identity is not easy to pin down in neat formulas. But we *hear* it in Lightfoot—in the tender strength of his voice, the lilt of his speech, and especially the balance of sincerity and restraint reflected in his lyrics and music. Perhaps this elusive quality of "Canadian identity" will emerge more clearly as we consider other songwriters and poets of our nation. We may also find in our survey that one key to the mystery of who we are may be our peculiar relation to *space*—both the space that surrounds us in this vast country and the "inner" space in which we feel our way toward personal significance and community.

There is no more natural starting point for this journey of self-discovery than Lightfoot's famous "Canadian Railroad Trilogy", a song cycle that conveys in one broad sweep the great expanse of our land that determines so much of our culture. Hearing Lightfoot's words and music gives us an awareness of what this landscape has meant to our ancestors and will continue to mean for their children. We can then see this meaning developed in detail in the works of major Canadian poets who, like Lightfoot, use the railroad as an image of our efforts to possess and comprehend our country.

Lightfoot's "Nous Vivons Ensemble" represents his attempt to deal with another kind of space that vitally affects Canadian history and culture—the gap between Québec and English Canada. His response to the growing challenge of Québec separatism is balanced here by works of Québec poets showing the aspirations of the Québecois and underscoring, perhaps, how great that gap really is.

Born in Orillia, Ontario, 1939, Lightfoot studied music at the Westlake School of Modern Music in Los Angeles, worked as a bank clerk for forty dollars a week, served as a chorus boy on CBC-TV's "Country Hoedown" show, and worked the Toronto bar circuit until the success of his songs drew attention to his possibilities as a performer. Up to now, he has recorded eight albums. He lives in Toronto with his Swedish wife, Brita, and their two children.

Canadian Railroad Trilogy

Gordon Lightfoot
Gordon Lightfoot, **Sunday Concert**, United Artists UAS 6714.
Copyright 1967 by M. Witmark & Sons.
Used by permission of Warner Bros. Music.
All rights reserved.

There was a time in this fair land when the railroad did not run,
When the wild majestic mountains stood alone against the sun,
Long before the white man and long before the wheel
When the green dark forest was too silent to be real.

But time has no beginnings and history has no bounds,
As to this verdant country they came from all around,
They sailed upon her waterways and they walked the forests tall,
Built the mines, the mills and the factories for the good of us all.

And when the young man's fancy was turnin' in the spring,
The railroad men grew restless for to hear the hammers ring,
Their minds were overflowin' with the visions of their day
And many a fortune won and lost and many a debt to pay.

For they looked in the future and what did they see,
They saw an iron road runnin' from the sea to the sea,
Bringin' the goods to a young, growin' land
All up from the seaports and into their hands.
"Look away!", said they, "across this mighty land,
From the eastern shore to the western strand!"

"Bring in the workers and bring up the rails,
We gotta lay down the tracks and tear up the trails,
Open her heart, let the life blood flow,
Gotta get on our way 'cause we're movin' too slow
Get on our way 'cause we're movin' too slow."

"Behind the blue rockies the sun is declinin',
The stars they come stealin' at the close of the day,
Across the wide prairie our loved ones lie sleeping
Beyond the dark ocean in a place far away."

"We are the navvies who work upon the railway,
Swingin' our hammers in the bright blazin' sun,

3

Livin' on stew and drinkin' bad whiskey,
Bendin' our backs 'til the long days are done."

"We are the navvies who work upon the railway,
Swingin' our hammers in the bright blazin' sun,
Layin' down track and buildin' the bridges,
Bendin' our backs 'til the railroad is done."

"So over the mountains and over the plains,
Into the muskeg and into the rain,
Up the Saint Lawrence all the way to Gaspé,
Swingin' our hammers and drawin' our pay,
Layin' 'em in and tyin' 'em down,
Away to the bunkhouse and into the town,
A dollar a day and a place for my head
A drink to the living, a toast to the dead!"

"Oh, the song of the future has been sung,
All the battles have been won,
On the mountain tops we stand,
All the world at our command.
We have opened up the soil
With our teardrops—
And our toil."

For there was a time in this fair land when the railroad did not run,
When the wild majestic mountains stood alone against the sun,
Long before the white man and long before the wheel,
When the green dark forest was too silent to be real
When the green dark forest was too silent to be real.
And many are the dead men,
Too silent
To be real.

from Tecumseh

Charles Mair

There was a time on this fair continent
When all things throve in spacious peacefulness.
The prosperous forests unmolested stood,
For where the stalwart oak grew there it lived
Long ages, and then died among its kind.
The hoary pines—those ancients of the earth—
Brimful of legends of the early world,
Stood thick on their own mountains unsubdued.
And all things else illumined by the sun,
Inland or by the lifted wave, had rest.
The passionate or calm pageants of the skies
No artist drew; but in the auburn west
Innumerable faces of fair cloud
Vanished in silent darkness with the day.
The prairie realm—vast ocean's paraphrase—
Rich in wild grasses numberless, and flowers
Unnamed save in mute Nature's inventory,
No civilized barbarian trenched for gain.
And all that flowed was sweet and uncorrupt,
The rivers and their tributary streams,
Undammed, wound on forever, and gave up
Their lonely torrents to weird gulfs of sea,
And ocean wastes unshadowed by a sail.

And all the wild life of this western world
Knew not the fear of man; yet in those woods,
And by those plenteous streams
        and mighty lakes,
And on stupendous steppes of peerless plain,
And in the rocky gloom of canyons deep,
Screened by the stony ribs of mountains hoar
Which steeped their snowy peaks
        in purging cloud,
And down the continent where tropic suns
Warmed to her very heart the mother earth,
And in the congeal'd north where silence self
Ached with intensity of stubborn frost,
There lived a soul more wild than barbarous;
A tameless soul—the sunburnt savage free—
Free, and untainted by the greed of gain:
Great Nature's man content
        with Nature's food.

The Precambrian Shield
from Towards the Last Spike

E.J. Pratt

On the North Shore a reptile lay asleep—
A hybrid that the myths might have conceived,
But not delivered, as progenitor
Of crawling, gliding things upon the earth.
She lay snug in the folds of a huge boa
Whose tail had covered Labrador and swished
Atlantic tides, whose body coiled itself
Around the Hudson Bay, then curled up north
Through Manitoba and Saskatchewan
To Great Slave Lake. In continental reach
The neck went past the Great Bear Lake until
Its head was hidden in the Arctic Seas.
This folded reptile was asleep or dead:
So motionless, she seemed stone dead—just seemed:
She was too old for death, too old for life,
For as if jealous of all living forms
She had lain there before bivalves began
To catacomb their shells on western mountains.
Somewhere within this life-death zone she sprawled,
Torpid upon a rock-and-mineral mattress.
Ice-ages had passed by and over her,
But these, for all their motion, had but sheared
Her spotty carboniferous hair or made
Her ridges stand out like the spikes of molochs.
Her back grown stronger every million years,
She had shed water by the longer rivers
To Hudson Bay and by the shorter streams
To the great basins to the south, had filled
Them up, would keep them filled until the end
Of Time. Was this the thing Van Horne set out
To conquer?

7

Cold Colloquy
from **Poem on Canada**

Patrick Anderson

What are you . . . ? they ask, in wonder.
And she replies in the worst silence of all her woods:
I am Candida with the cane wind.

What are you . . . ? they ask again, their mouths full of gum,
their eyes full of the worst silence of the worst winter in a hundred years
and the frames of their faces chipped round the skaters' picture—

What are you . . .? they ask.
And she replies: I am the wind that wants a flag.
I am the mirror of your picture
until you make me the marvel of your life.
Yes, I am one and none, pin and pine, snow and slow,
America's attic, an empty room,
a something possible, a chance, a dance
that is not danced. A cold kingdom.

Are you a dominion of them? they ask, scurrying
home on streetcars, skiing the hill's shoulder
and hurrying where the snow is heaping colder and colder.
Are you a dominion of them? they ask.
Most loyal and empirical, she says, in ice ironic,
and subject of the king's most gratuitous modesty, she says.
What do you do then?
Lumbering is what I do and whitening is what I wheat,
but I am full of hills and sadness;
snow is where I drift and wave my winds
and as silence my doom, distance is my dream.
Mine are the violet tones of the logs in rivers,
my tallness is the tallness of the pines and the grain elevators
tubular by the scarps of coal, at Quebec.

My caves are the caves of ice but also the holes of Cartier
where the poor squat, numb with winter,
and my poverty is their rags and the prairies' drought.

What is the matter then . . .? they ask, and some are indifferent,
What is the matter then . . .? they ask.

The matter is the sections and the railways, she replies,
and the shouting lost by the way and the train's whistle
like wild-life in the night.
The matter is the promise that was never taken, she replies,
above your heads the cool and giant air
and the future aching round you like an aura—
land of the last town and the distant point,
land of the lumber track losing itself
petering out in the birches, the half-wish
turning back in the wastes of winter or slums
and the skiers lovely and lonely upon the hills
rising in domes of silence. The matter is
the skiers, she replies, athletically lonely,
drowsed in their delight, who hunt and haunt
the centres of their silence and excitement:
finding the cirrus on the high sierras
sluice down the dangers of their dear content—
the matter is being lost in a dream of motion
as larks are in their lights, or bees and flies
glued on the humpbacked honey of summertime.

What should we do then, what should we do . . .? they ask,
out of the factories rattling a new war,
on all the Sundays time has rocked to motion.
What should we do then . . .? they ask, English and French,
Ukrainians, Poles, Finns, at drugstore corners
of streets extended to the ultimate seas
of their defended but ambiguous city.

—Suffer no more the vowels of Canada
to speak of miraculous things with a cleft palate—
let the Canadian,
with glaciers in his hair, straddle the continent,
in full possession of his earth and north
dip down his foot and touch the New York lights
or stir the vegetable matter of the Bahamas
within the Carib gutter. Let
the skiers go with slogans of their eyes
to crowd a country whose near neighbourhood's
the iron kindness of the Russian coasts—
through deserts of snow or dreary wastes of city,
the empty or the emptily crowded North.

And see, she says, the salmon pointing home
from the vast sea, the petalled plethora
and unplumbed darkness of the sea, she says:
gliding along their silvery intuitions
like current on its cables, volt upon volt,
to flash at last, sparking the mountain falls
of Restigouche—spawning a silver million.

Transcontinental

Earle Birney

Crawling across this sometime garden
now in our trainbeds like clever nits
in a plush caterpilllar should we take time
to glance from our dazzle of magazines
and behold this great green girl grown sick
with man   sick with the likes of us?

Toes mottled long ago by soak of seaports
ankles rashed with stubble
belly papulous with stumps?
And should we note where maggoting miners
still bore her bones to feed our crawling host
or consider the scars across her breasts
the scum of tugs upon her lakeblue eyes
the clogging logs within her blood—
in the doze between our magazines?

For certainly she is ill   her skin
is creased with our coming and going
and we trail in her face the dark breath of her dooming

She is too big and strong perhaps to die
of this disease but she grows quickly old
this lady   old with us—
nor have we any antibodies for her aid
except our own.

—1945

The Canadian

bill bissett

On the train, back from th Empress
dining car, snowing woodlands
, pulling thru Manitoba, recall
   how sum yrs after th second centenary
of th founding of Halifax, which
   date I commemorated with sign
   above my father's street door,
   into two parts i divided, th half
on th left, what once was, before
1749, th MicMac Indian, th second
half, after that time, a British sailor,
on board, telescope to eye, sailing
   into harbour, Montbatten drove by
   my father's house that day, part of
th ceremonies, dressed by University gown
   & cap, later that year, th woman to be
   Queen, then Princess Elizabeth drove
     thru Halifax town, in bullet-proof car.

     But i was to recall, as i did,
   coming back from th dining car, that
   sum yrs. after Halifax had her bicentenary,
   i wrote my third or fourth pome, in
   which, constructed as allegory, i did en
   vision th society of fact in Canada
as a train, its peopuls classd, & sub-
classed, according to th rank & station,
that is, what they cud claim they owned, or,
who they could claim owned them, its
peopuls cut off from each other by
       such coach cars and compartments.

And i recall, part of th allegory was
thc train going thru th tunnel—darkness,
fortifying the condition, keeping each in place,
lest they overcome fear & th structure toppul.

It's not such a good allegory, my
friends sd—well, now that sum of my best
friends are in jail—i see its uses,
my boyhood despair—seeing, as th
train rolls thru Manitoba, how it
does seem that still peopul are hungry in
this country, sum of my best friends are
hungry, peopul are hungry, they hunger
for food—outside of this train there is
no food—in it there is good & bad food;
food that will just keep yu strong enuff
to keep yr place—food that is
just good enuff yu dream
of better food—and food that is so good
yu become encouraged to accept
that this train is not going to crash
cannot be changed, from within
or without, is God or Allah's very
handiwork, but where is th food
on this train, this one
to show me Allah in all things,
for then, in ourselves th best food,
we share th bounty
on this Iron Horse.

Chosen Fate

Margaret Hagerty
Thessalon High School
Thessalon, Ontario

If fate was mine to choose
I would lift this country
And embrace it in my arms
And mold it in my hands
And
Shake it up
And
Toss it round
And I would tell
That proud American eagle
To fly away somewhere
And thumb my nose
At some high official
Riding past with an artificial smile
Pasted on his plastic face
And I would stretch my arms to the sky
And shout "Hey World I love you!"
But if someone should hear me
I'd be afraid of dying.

Nous Vivons Ensemble:

We've Got to Stay Together

Gordon Lightfoot
Gordon Lightfoot, **The Summer Side of Life**, Warner Bros. Canada, MS 2037.
Copyright 1971 Early Morning Music.

Nous vivons ensemble,
Nous nous connaissons maintenant,
Voici comment nous pouvons découvrir une autre humanité.

Sur les Plaines d'Abraham,
Lors du dernier sacrifice,
Toi et moi, nous dormions très loin dans le temps,
Souviens toi des enfants qui attendent encore.

Si tu me veux, je serai là,
C'est tout ce que j'ai à dire,
Car comprend moi, je ne suis pas sourd
À la musique que tu joues.

      ● ● ●

We've got to stay together,
We've got to find each other now,
That is how we can learn all about the other man's song.

On the Plains of Abraham,
When they set the lamb to die,
You and I were asleep in the Rock of Ages,
Remember the unborn children still to come.

If you need me then I need you,
There's nothin' else needs sayin',
Understand it, I'm not too deaf
To hear the song you're playin'.

October

Gaston Miron
translated by Fred Cogswell

The man of our time has a face of flagellation
and you, Land of Quebec, Mother Courage
you are big
with our sooty sorrowful dreams
and an endless drain of bodies and souls

I was born your son
in your worn-out mountains of the north
I ache and suffer
bitten by that birth
yet in my arms my youth is glowing

here are my knees
may our world forgive us
we have allowed our fathers to be humbled in spirit
we have allowed the light of the world to be debased
to the shame and self-contempt of our brothers
we could not bind the roots of our suffering
into the universal sorrow of each degraded man

I go to join the burning company
whose struggle shares and breaks the bread of the common lot
in the quicksands of a common grief

we will make you, Land of Quebec
a bed of resurrections
and in the myriad lightnings of our transformations
in this leaven of ours from which the future is rising
in our uncompromising will
men will hear your pulse beating in history
this is ourselves rippling in the autumn of October
this is the russet sound of deer in the light
the future free and easy

Your Country

Gatien Lapointe
translated by John Glassco

If you will open your eyes
And if you will lay your hands
On the snow, the birds, the trees, the beasts,
Patiently, softly,
With all the weight of your heart;

If you will take time by the hand
And look upon the land
Patiently, softly;

If you will recognize your people
And if you recognize the pain
Trembling upon the background of their eyes;

If you will write the words love and loneliness
Patiently, gently,
On every season, every house;

If you will name bread, blood, day, night
And that wild unalterable desire
Burning at the heart of all things;

If you will take every death of your childhood
Patiently, softly, in your arms,
With all the strength of your despair:

Then your country can be born.

Guy

Sylvia Frank
London Central Collegiate Institute
London, Ontario

Black hair and beard
Pale complexion
Small but solid.
Rimbaud accompanied him,
Wearing red and yellow.
When I saw him,
My mind would stop to think
Of Quebec and independent people.

I opened his locker this morning,
It was empty,
Except for a crumpled
Piece of paper.
I thought maybe he had left a note,
Like a husband leaving his wife,
But he hadn't.

Chilliwack

2

In Lightfoot's "Nous Vivons Ensemble" and the poems of Gaston Miron and Gatien Lapointe, we see the political dimension of our greatest Canadian problem: communication. As previously suggested, it is a problem of space. In this section, we see how the problem affects us personally—how the vastness of Canada, at once our glory and our challenge, is mirrored in the spaces between and within us, the result being loneliness, pride, and sometimes an intense need for intimacy. "Rain-o", one of Chilliwack's finest songs, lightly touches on these things. Red Lane and Milton Acorn show, in their very different ways, what poetry can do to illuminate the long corridors separating us all.

For the past four years, Chilliwack has been the leading rock group in the Vancouver area. Originally known as the Collectors, Chilliwack has now several albums to its credit and may be helping to create a distinctive Canadian West Coast sound. Bill Henderson, Claire Lawrence, and Ross Turney are the anchormen.

Rain-O

Bill Henderson
Chilliwack, Parrot/London PAS 71040.
Reprinted by permission of The Collectors Music Corporation Ltd.

Rain-o, rain-o fall upon the earth again and make it good
Make it cool and fill the river
Fill the pool and quench the thirst
Of every fool and every sage
And every sour soul who's lost so much
He doesn't know his need.

In vain, in vain, I tell you that we're all the same
'Cause there you stand a-sayin', "Man, it's not for real,"
'Cause we're the ones who get to steal the show
And I don't know,
I guess you're right
But even so
If there's no audience
There just ain't no show.

Rain-o, rain, won't you fall on me again
Because a moldy mold has settled on my brain.

In vain, in vain, I tell you that we're all the same
'Cause there you stand a-sayin', "Man, it's not for real,"
'Cause we're the ones who get to steal the show
And I don't know,
I guess you're right
But even so
If there's no audience
There just ain't no show.

Marchlands V

Red Lane

Walking the road to town
an old truck stops by me
and a man looks out at me

    "Where you headed, kid?"
    town probably
    needs a haircut

"Town"
what a stupid lookin hat

    thought so
    "Climb in!"
    what the hell is he grinnin at
    "Going that way myself."

climb in!
"I'd rather walk."
if it's okay with you

    "Walk?"
    well of all the . . .
    "Well walk then!"
    ungrateful . . .

"I will"
and you know it

    that's for sure
    "You bet your life."

"And don't we all?"
now there's a line

what the hell
"If you say so."
hah

"And don't we all?"
hah

"Hah!"
hah
"You got a lot to learn."
by God

"And don't we all?"
hahahaha

"Hah!"
what am I doing
sitting here arguing
with this . . .
"Well . . ."
well . . .
"Enjoy your walk."
two and a half miles kid
and a cold wind blowin

I will
"Enjoy your ride."

that's for sure
"You bet your life."

"And don't we all?"
and . . .

"Go to hell!"
And meshing gears
and spinning wheels
away went the man in the truck

A way he went

. . .and don't we all

and don't we all

"And don't we all!"

Dialogue
andante con moto

Garry Cardinal
Salisbury Composite High School
Sherwood Park, Alberta

"-mommy! he's all bent and *broken*!-"
"-but consider the problem in-"
"-ooh that's *very good*-"
"-come *on*, KITTY!-"
"-on his *own* trip-"
"-and now the time is come-"
"-well if you don't *like it* in this-"
"-like *I* say, never say die-"

"-so it was like this-"
"-oh! ex*cuse me*-"
"-phase inversion-"
"-and it begins on-"
"-you really must have liked her-"
"-nobody sang at *my* birthday-"
"-fromage please, cheese-"
Yeah-

Kiss

Milton Acorn

The twist, the bend or arching up
to kiss, always includes—with me
, a watching of myself. It's a stepping
into strangeness, becoming the man
of hoped-for truth, who moves in the blood.

Was it so with Judas? The step towards
the man moving in grace, the clutch
and the shape his body took, lips leading
. . .was it felt? Was the betrayal
felt as if two men, the mover and the motion
were there, balanced in the walk and the stop?

It's a ceasing to be the dry grainy self
of affairs, the bringing of another
into the arm's loop, the compass
the body contains for itself. Like
receiving a kiss, it's the new breath
of a new spirit, allowed by yours
in the presence you carry . . .and a living guess
included in your memories, hopes and urges.

A new complexion of colors. The god (the thing
out there that's the tone of kindness) comes down
for you both, into you both. Two people stand
for a wonderful one, as if it were a new person.

I'm thinking of a sudden kiss I got from
a stranger I'd been watching, and thus knew
she'd been watching me . . . in a crazy coffee house
where she used to come and go dancing
from table to table, kissing all
she acknowledged part of the company
. . . a contract to love and be loved.

Thus it'll be when the last rabbi crowns
the Messiah . . . It'll be a kiss
he's topped with, and all enraptured souls
will kiss and joyfully allow each other to exist.

Bruce Cockburn

3

As Milton Acorn suggests in his poem, "The Kiss", space need not only separate people. It can also exist as a clearing ground where we can discover one another. In the following songs, Bruce Cockburn develops this insight in lovely, delicate structures of words and music. To appreciate them, the listener must grant him absolute silence, the equivalent of space in sound. Then he will hear how both the form and content of Cockburn's songs reflect this strange power of distance to create not just frustration, but also its very opposite: perfect intimacy.

What we are dealing with here is yet another aspect of "space" in Canadian culture—the Canadian artist's respect for *aesthetic* space as *living* room. Cockburn tries to explain it this way:

"Space may be a misleading word because it is so vague in relation to music, but maybe it has to do with Canadians being more involved with the space around them rather than trying to fill it up as the Americans do. I mean physical space and how it makes you feel about yourself. Media clutter may follow. All of it a kind of greed. The more Canadians fill up their space the more they will be like Americans. We seem to take it so much for granted. Perhaps because our urban landscapes are not yet deadly, and because they seem accidental to the whole expanse of the land."*

Cockburn (pronounced "Coburn") was born in Ottawa in 1945. As a child he learned to love nature from his farmer grandfather. After high school, he studied music at the Berklee School of Music, worked as a street musician in Paris, and now has three albums, each representing a further musical and poetic advance. In my own view, he stands with Joni Mitchell and Leonard Cohen as among the finest song-writers of our land.

*Myrna Kostash, "The Pure, Uncluttered Spaces of Bruce Cockburn", *Saturday Night*, June 1972, p. 24.

25

Happy Good Morning Blues

Bruce Cockburn
Bruce Cockburn, **High Winds White Sky**,
True North (Columbia) TN 3.
Copyright Golden Mountain Music (BMI Canada).

Good day to you
fat balloon man
may you always have air
you sing a song everybody can believe.

Good day to you
uncle tom cat
out to trick the whole world
you carry a tune for nobody but yourself.

Bonjour à toi
herr policeman
may your boots always fit
someday you'll find a song you can believe.

Good morning good people
the sun is long sailing
the only clouds you see
are carried within
soon they'll be blown all away
wind gonna rise and blow those clouds away
wind gonna rise and blow your blues away
your sun gonna shine in my back door
    some day . . .

Legend of the Morning

Paul Chamberland
translated by John Glassco

Today,

you will forget to be afraid

fear may whiten the prisoner's temples, you will
    not be afraid
you will see that memory has
    become an endless surface, a depth of the resins
    the atoms and the salts crying out under the
    tread of Noon

Today,

on the children's fingers are spinning

               magnetic Sundays
               holidays of sugar
               light itself

Today,

the horizon is table of meals and marvels
bed of amorous delay
lawn with the blue depths of childhood
pert little miracles

               daffodils
               glittering mica
               snakes
               catbirds
               whitethroats

the scaffoldings of dawn perfume the future

wood is good
water is pure

        the garden of cool hands revolves
        young mothers in a tizzy
        rings of nylon
        sunflowers
        silken hysteria

we hear the rivers brawl
the barrage resound

the hormone spawns its miracles

            rainbow trouts
            golden globes
            cloudbursts of crystal

hidden salt quivers at the joyous quick
symphonic altitudes
stairs of odours
and the oil of winter games

we dream the lovely sea
with its cabins of softest moss

we dream

        of the chords lips make in the
          forests
        the twinkling of winds
        the merry-go-rounds of noon
        the runways into space

we dream

You Point to the Sky

Bruce Cockburn
Bruce Cockburn, **High Winds White Sky**,
True North (Columbia) TN 3.
Copyright Golden Mountain Music (BMI Canada).

You point to the sky
the sky
is reflected in your eyes
and i
want to fly
        on a carpet of brown leaves
        we retrace the steps of change
        construct a tapestry of what will come.

You point to the sea
i see
what seems to be so free
bound by
empty sky
        on a tower of gray earth
        far above the spray-struck stone
        we climb toward the melting point of time.

● ● ●

here we tumble down the path
comic beggars trading laughs
for scraps from the tables of the wise.

The Natural Thing

bp Nichol

i go out at night
when the moon is new
hair grown long
and pockets full of poems

i carry strange birds on my shoulders
that sing and cry
thru the long night

walk with angels
when the wind is high
wings billowing around me
and long robes flowing

i am a stranger in the new fields
writing poems
from natural things

i gather
stars moon trees and rivers
shape them in my hands
as they urge me

'till they foam forth
a new
more natural thing

I, Icarus

Alden Nowlan

There was a time when I could fly. I swear it.
Perhaps, if I think for a moment, I can even tell you the year.
My room was on the ground floor at the rear of the house.
My bed faced a window.
Night after night I lay on my bed and willed myself to fly.
It was hard work, I can tell you.
Sometimes I lay perfectly still for an hour before I felt my body rising from the bed.
I rose slowly, slowly until I floated three or four feet above the floor.
Then, with a kind of swimming motion, I propelled myself toward the window.

Outside, I rose higher and higher, above the pasture fence, above the clothesline,
    above the dark, haunted trees beyond the pasture.
And, all the time, I heard the music of flutes.
It seemed the wind made this music.
And sometimes there were voices singing.

Let Us Go Laughing

Bruce Cockburn
Bruce Cockburn, **High Winds White Sky**,
True North (Columbia) TN 3.
Copyright Golden Mountain Music
(BMI Canada).

My canoe lies on the water
evening holds the bones of day
the sun like gold dust slips away

One by one antique stars
herald the arrival of
their pale protectress moon

Ragged branches vibrate
strummed by winds from o'er the hill
singing tales of ancient days

Far and silent lightning
stirs the cauldron of the sky
i turn my bow toward the shore.

• • •

As we grow out of stones
on and on and on
so we'll all go to bones
on and on for many a year
   but let us go laughing-o
   let us go

And may the holy hermit's staff
on and on and on
guide you to the shortest path
on and on for many a year
   and let us go laughing-o
   let us go.

Song to the Wanderer

Traditional Haida* Indian Poem
translated by Hermia Harris Fraser

I cannot stay, I cannot stay!
I must take my canoe and fight the waves,
For the Wanderer spirit is seeking me.

The beating of great, black wings on the sun,
The Raven has stolen the ball of the sun,
From the Kingdom of Light he has stolen the sun.

I cannot stay, I cannot stay!
The Raven has stolen the Child of the Chief,
Of the Highest Chief in the Kingdom of Light.

The Slave Wife born from the first clam shell
Is in love with the boy who was stolen away,
The lovers have taken the Raven's fire.

The Slave who was born from the first clam shell
Has made love to the wife who was born from the shell,
This Slave man has stolen her treasures away.

He is the Wanderer spirit who calls me,
He is the One who has charge of the birds,
He is the One who loves plants, beasts, and fish.

I am the one who loves the wild woods,
I am the one who embraces the sea.
I must take my canoe and escape tonight!

* "Haida" is the popular name for the Skittagetan Indians
of Queen Charlotte Islands, British Columbia.

31

Fragments: Beach

Margaret Atwood

1
At first we know
we intrude, like thrown
bottles, junk metal

but the place grinds us

piece of glass we
found, turned by the
stones into a stone

2
We arrange the beach, build
a driftwood hut out of the empty
huts; the fallen
walls teach us
how to build
             we pack
barricades of sand

which blows into
blankets, shoes, our tight
containers
           the beach
           arranges us

3
the tent a
skin stretched over
our eyes is a new
sense
        lets in
grass noises rasping, weed-
taste of mist, shiver
of early moon, a different
light

4
In the afternoon the sun
expands, we enter
its hot perimeter
                our feet
burn, our hair lifts
incandescent, the waves
are chill fire, clean
us to bone

5
the surf scours our ears

wind bends
the sand around us

the shapes we make
in the sand from lying down
are salt, are brown, are
flesh

6
light is a sound
                it roars
it fills us
        we swell with it
are strenuous, vast

rocks

hurl our voices / we

are abolished

7
In the night the tents
the driftwood
walls, the sleepers

lose their hold
on shore, are drawn
out on a gigantic tide

we also make the slow deep
circle
        until
the sea returns us

leaves us
absolved, washed
shells on the morning beach

Dead Man's Song
Dreamed by One Who is Alive

Traditional Eskimo Poem

I am filled with joy
When the day peacefully dawns
Up over the heavens.
I am filled with joy
When the sun slowly rises
Up over the heavens.

But else I choke with fear
At greedy maggot throngs;
They eat their way in
At the bottom of my collarbone
And in my eyes.

Here I lie, recollecting
How stifled with fear I was
When they buried me
In a snow hut out on the lake.

A block of snow was pushed to,
Incomprehensible it was
How my soul should make its way
And fly to the game land up there

The door-block worried me,
And even greater grew my fear
When the fresh-water ice split in the cold
And the frost-crack thunderously grew
Up over the heavens.

Glorious was life
In winter,
But did winter bring me joy?
No! Ever was I so anxious

For sole-skins and skins for kamiks.
Would there be enough for us all?
Yes, I was ever anxious.

Glorious was life
In summer,
But did summer bring me joy?
No! Ever was I so anxious
For skins and rugs for the platform
Yes, I was ever anxious.

Glorious was life
When standing at one's fishing hole
On the ice.
But did standing at the fishing hole bring me joy?
No! Ever was I so anxious
For my tiny little fishhook
If it should not get a bite.

Glorious was life
When dancing in the dance-house,
But did dancing in the dance-house bring me joy?
No! Ever was I so anxious,
That I could not recall
The song I was to sing.
Yes, I was ever anxious.

Glorious was life . . .
Now I am filled with joy
For every time a dawn
Makes white the sky of night,
For every time the sun goes up
Over the heavens.

33

Maniac

Rochelle Kahn
R.S. McLaughlin Collegiate and Vocational Institute
Oshawa, Ontario

no
    I cannot believe the maniac fishwoman
        she belies your depth
                creases your apron with her useless hands
        as blind as the bass who spits out his life
                    into her aching lap.

No
    I cannot believe the ranting sweep
        whose dustblackened feet
                stepped through your chimney
        to gather your firemist and now weeps
                    over an empty bucket.

NO
    they are all insane!
                the deafman did not hear you go
                    sighing

See
    you are Here
           still
    I can feel you
    I can see yo
    I can hear y

NO!
    you have only slipped away for more wine.

Shining Mountain

Bruce Cockburn
Bruce Cockburn, **High Winds White Sky**, True North (Columbia) TN 3.
Copyright Golden Mountain Music (BMI Canada).

I went up on the mountain side
to see what i could see
to see what i could be
on the shining mountain.

I watched the day go down in fire
and sink in the valley
and sink into the sea
drown in golden fire.

Fireflies danced in the forest night
the trees began to sing
the crags began to sing
above the black forest.

I went up on the mountain side
to know what i did know
to know whence i did know
on the crowning mountain.

Wabanaki Song

Traditional Indian Song
translated by Mrs. Wallace Brown

Come, my *moo sarge*,* let us go up that shining mountain, and sit
together on that shining mountain; there we will watch the
beautiful sun go down from the shining mountain.
There we will sit, till the beautiful night traveller arises above the
shining mountain; we will watch him, as he climbs to the
beautiful skies.
We will also watch the little stars following their chief.
We will also watch the northern lights playing their game of
ball in their cold, shiny country.
There we will sit, on the beautiful mountain, and listen to the
thunder beating his drum.
We will see the lightning when she lights her pipe.
We will see the great whirlwind running a race with *betchi-vesay*.**
There we will sit, 'til every living creature feels like sleeping.
There we will hear the great owl sing his usual song, *teeg-lee-
goo-wul-tique*, and see all the animals obey his song.
There we will sit on that beautiful mountain, and watch the little
stars in their sleepless flight. They do not mind the song,
teeg-lee-goo-wul-tique; neither will we mind it, but sit more
closely together, and think of nothing but ourselves, on the
beautiful mountain.
Again, the *teeg-lee-goo-wul-tique* will be heard, and the night
traveller will come closer to warn us that all are dreaming,
except ourselves and the little stars. They and their chief are
coursing along, and our minds go with them. Then the owl
sleeps; no more is heard *teeg-lee-goo-wul-tique*; the lightning
ceases smoking; the thunder ceases beating his drum; and
though we feel inclined to sleep, yet will we sit on the
beautiful, shining mountain.

*moo sarge: Wabanaki
term of endearment.

**betchi-vesay: squall.

36

ode to frank silvera

bill bissett

yu might think that moving
silently thru th tenement
yr holsters bright nd lively
in th yellow colord air

yu might think that yr horse
kickin without sound at th moon
where sum say th faild souls
those who cant find bodies hang
out

yu might say movin soft on top
of eggshells tord yr path, karma
is will plus fate, th old time
blend

yu might hope there is sum one
to love yu at th end of th road
yu might see nothin can grow in
th dust of yr anxieties

yu might say that fate is whats left
aftr yu do nothing. yu can go on
alone with all th mysteries of bing.

yu walk out of th town at sun rise
before there is sound th fields
maybe yu get rheumatism from too
much mornin dew maybe yr hungr gets
too deep to drink maybe yr holsters
get parchd maybe theres only silence

yu might say there is always
more love of dark and golden being

yu might say yul fly
more like th crow

yu cud say yu dont have to kill
yrself that'l be taken care of

yu cud say th mountain and love is
hard and eternal. never yields to
nothing. sumtime yu are th wind
racing green ovr th hairy fields

sumtimes yu are th blind eye
of th sun turning in yr belly

yu dream

yu move further out a town

Conversation

Frederik Wendt
Hants West Rural High School
Ellershouse, Nova Scotia

I said man is foremost among animals
And the trees chuckled
I said let life persist
And the mountains rumbled
I said long live the earth
And the stars roared with such a laughter
That I became deaf
So I could hear the sunrise

Willie Dunn

4

Paradoxically, the Canadian feeling for space, that flowers in
the delicate sensitivity of poets like Bruce Cockburn, also provides a distinctively Canadian way of perpetuating social injus-
tice. The most striking example is our treatment of the Indians.
Instead of directly persecuting the peoples who once owned
this country, we simply set them aside, not only by means
of "reservations", but also by putting such a distance between
them and our national concerns that we generally forget they
even exist.

Now, however, a voice has arisen from the Indian people that
will profoundly disturb this comfortable distancing. Willie Dunn,
born in the Restigouche Reserve of Quebec in 1941, sings
the life of the Indian people so eloquently, simply and powerfully
that increasing numbers of Canadians are finding it impossible
to turn away any longer from what he represents. Dunn has
also underscored his portrait of the Indian condition in a remarkable film he made for the Canadian National Film Board. It
is called "The Ballad of Crowfoot", and the lyrics of the title
song are reprinted in *Truth and Fantasy,* eds. Homer Hogan
and Kenneth Weber (Agincourt, Ontario: Methuen, 1972).

Charlie*

Willie Dunn
Willie Dunn, Kotai Productions/London.
Copyright. Reprinted with permission of White Roots of Peace, a North American
Indian communications group, Mohawk Nation, via Rooseveltown, N.Y., and
Willie Dunn.

Refrain:
Walk on, little Charlie,
Walk on through the snow,
Headin' down the railway line,
Tryin' to make it home,
And he's made it forty miles,
Six hundred left to go.
It's a long, old lonesome journey,
Shufflin' through the snow.

He's so lonesome and he's hungry,
It's been some time since last he's ate,
And as the night grows colder,
He wonders of his fate,
For his legs are racked with pain
As he staggers through the night,
As he sees through his troubled eyes,
His hands are turning white.

Lonely as a single star
In the skies above,
His father in a mining camp,
His mother in the ground,
And he's lookin' for his dad,
And he's lookin' out for love,
Just a lost little boy by the railroad track
Moving homeward bound.

Is that the Great Windigo**
Come to look upon my face?
And are the stars explodin'
Down misty aisles of space,
And who's that comin' down the track,
Walkin' up to me,
Her arms outstretched and waitin',
Waitin' just for me?

Refrain

*This song is based on the true story of Charlie W_____, an Indian
boy who ran away from a "residential" school in the far north, trying
to get back to his tribal village. He followed the railroad tracks for
forty miles before freezing to death.

**The Great Windigo:* An evil spirit, sometimes in the form of an ice giant,
whose appearance can make men mad or drive them to cannibalism. Belief
in this being still persists among some Ojibwa and Cree Indians.

Thoughts on Silence

Mary Jane Sterling

What am I doing here
Among these strange people
Sitting in these funny desks
Staring at this paper?
Oh yes, I am in school.
These people are my classmates.
Though they chatter all the time
They are silent now.
Now I can think.
I see a bird flying high in the air.
Maybe it is flying south.
My heart leaps with the bird
Taking a message to my mother.
My mind is heavy, thinking something sad has
Happened at home.
But the birds are singing
Everything is all right.
The breeze has whispered something in my ear.
I hope it whispers the same joyous words to my people.
I get lonely for my family and I especially miss my mother
But I shall see them all soon.
When we meet we won't even touch hands
But our hearts will leap with joy
And in our minds we will be glad.

The Last Crackle

Gordon Williams

She sat there by the west window
Unmindful of the mosquitoes who'd always
Manage to squeeze thru the screen mesh
Insect barrier. Now it was sunset
Again, so many days of waiting.

A long time ago there were hardly
Any bearded men, now the forests are full!
They've flung bridges across all our rivers
And even our lakes. The sky is filled with metal
Birds that make noise loud as thunder.

All our men are dead and our young ones
Have no ambition. They took it all away,
Those bearded men, with their strange ways,
"Kneel with us" they said, "and pray!"
Then they took our land and children.

Now they've taken their beards off and shorn their
Hair, and they smile quick as a rattler's strike;
Before you open your door, a face of stone,
Then before your door is fully open, a smile
Trying to sell an old woman beauty cosmetics.

Her eyes were closed, she seemed to be asleep
Her drifting took her back a hundred years or more to
When she was just a little girl throwing pebbles making ripples
On the water's picture of white poplar trees.
Her days of waiting were ended, her chair
Rocking her away, and the last rays washing her face,
While the chair gave away the last crackle.

Broker*

Willie Dunn
Willie Dunn, Kotai Productions/London.
Copyright. Reprinted with permission of White Roots of Peace,
a North American Indian communications group,
Mohawk Nation, via Rooseveltown, N.Y., and Willie Dunn.

Hey there, broker, pawn my watch,
It won't stay with me without the chain,
Without the clouds you won't have the rain,
Pick it up, now it's gone.

You've taken my land and my living too,
And left me standing with nothing to do,
Threw back some blankets and a welfare check,
Without no regard, no self respect,

Here I stand in a brand new school,
Government's still talking about the cost,
But I'm still looking for something I lost,
Old men live, and they're gone.

Hey there, preacher, with the long robes on,
When you robbed my soul, you did me wrong,
You've gone and taken my old heart's song,
And gave me something back that don't belong.

Build a bridge of tempered steel,
To span the windy depth of time,
Remove the base, the bridge will fall,
Into the fires below.

Hey there, broker, pawn my watch,
It won't stay with me without the chain,
Without the clouds, you won't have the rain,
Pick it up and be gone.

*"Broker" is the term used for the government
official who distributes cheques to reservation Indians.

I Was Mixing Stars and Sand

Sarain Stump

I was mixing stars and sand
In front of him
But he couldn't understand
I was keeping the lightning of
The thunder in my purse
Just in front of him
But he couldn't understand
And I had been killed a thousand times
Right at his feet
But he hadn't understood

Pride

Pat Burke
Joseph Burr Tyrrell High School
Fort Smith, North West Territories

Once we had pride.
Where did it go?
We loved our land;
Pure as fallen snow.

Then we were trod upon
Broken and shorn.
We gave up land and home,
And the pride of being born.

Today we are different,
Almost destroyed,
But pride grows within us
We aren't white mens' toys.

Someday before our culture dies,
Our hearts will grow,
We'll say with pride
I AM AN INDIAN.

Of Pride In Race
—Written In Anger

Barry Ahenakew,
 Prince Albert Collegiate Institute
Canwood, Saskatchewan

Pride.
What has it done for me?
What has it done for others?
God. I wish you'd tell me.
Is it worth it?
Pride's a curse,
A curse of all races.
I'm proud to be a person,
A living healthy thing.
God. How I wish
All the people would be
Like this.
Maybe I'm wrong.
Maybe I should be proud,
Wear a leather outfit
All the time
With braids and the works,
But time has passed—
What's the use,
What would it do for me?
Now today.
Not yesterday.

A Lament For Confederation

Chief Dan George

How long have I known you, Oh Canada? A hundred years? Yes, and many many *seelanum** more. And today, when you celebrate your hundred years, Oh Canada, I am sad for all the Indian people throughout the land.

For I have known you when your forests were mine; when they gave me my meat and my clothing. I have known you in your streams and rivers where your fish flashed and danced in the sun, where the waters said come, come and eat of my abundance. I have known you in the freedom of your winds. And my spirit, like the winds, once roamed your good lands.

But in the long hundred years since the white man came, I have seen my freedom disappear like the salmon going mysteriously out to sea. The white man's strange customs which I could not understand, pressed down upon me until I could no longer breathe.

When I fought to protect my land and my home, I was called a savage. When I neither understood nor welcomed this way of life, I was called lazy. When I tried to rule my people, I was stripped of my authority.

My nation was ignored in your history textbooks—they were little more important in the history of Canada than the buffalo that ranged the plains. I was ridiculed in your plays and motion pictures, and when I drank your firewater I got drunk—very, very drunk. And I forgot.

Oh Canada, how can I celebrate with you this centenary, this hundred years? Shall I thank you for the reserves that are left me of my beautiful forests? For the canned fish of my rivers? For the loss of my pride and authority, even among my own people? For the lack of my will to fight back? No! I must forget what's past and gone.

Oh God in Heaven! Give me back the courage of the olden Chiefs. Let me wrestle with my surroundings. Let me again, as in the days of old, dominate my environment. Let me humbly accept this new culture and through it rise up and go on.

Oh God! Like the Thunderbird of old I shall rise again out of the sea; I shall grab the instruments of the white man's success—his education, his skills, and with these new tools I shall build my race into the proudest segment of your society. Before I follow the great chiefs who have gone before us, Oh Canada, I shall see these things come to pass.

I shall see our young braves and our chiefs sitting in the houses of law and government, ruling and being ruled by the knowledge and freedoms of *our* great land. So shall we shatter the barriers of our isolation. So shall the *next* hundred years be the greatest in the proud history of our tribes and nations.

*Squamish word for "year" used by Indians living in North Vancouver and Burrard Inlet.

for Joe MacKinaw

Jim Dumont

In my youth
I went south,
In my dreams
I went south.

There
I watched them hunt . . .
I watched them hunt the buffalo.
And in my heart
I hunted with them.

Now they are gone.
The buffalo have left,
Ashamed,
That we had let them die,
Mercilessly,
At the hand of the white hunters.

But our real suffering
Has not yet come upon us.
Soon there will be great destruction.
Fire will cover the whole land.
We will be punished.

This is the truth;
There will be much suffering.
The old people tell us that:
The Great Spirit has talked with them.
The old people know;
There has been too much evil.

Yet there is a little hope,
The Great Spirit makes room for goodness.

A young boy will come
The old people say,
And he will lead those who know goodness;
He will lead them into the mountains
No whiteman has been there;
No whiteman knows;
Destruction will not be allowed there;
And there is the sanctuary for goodness.

. . . in my old age
I will go in dreams
And I will find the buffalo again.

The Guess Who

5

According to Ritchie York in *Axes, Chops, and Hot Licks* (Edmonton: M. G. Hurtig Ltd., 1971), The Guess Who was the Canadian rock group whose success was so great in the United States that Canadian rock stations finally began paying attention to their own musicians. The Guess Who is one of the leaders of the new Rock Revolution—the musical protest of the human organism against all those forces in modern society that try to manipulate, mechanize, and mutilate it. "Share the Land", "Hand Me Down World", and "Bus Rider" are some of the strongest expressions of this revolt, and the accompanying poems show how Canadian poets share this same concern. Archibald Lampman's poem, "Freedom", written in the nineteenth century, also demonstrates that the Guess Who is actually carrying on an old tradition of Canadian poet-warriors who fight to keep the connection between man and nature.

Enormously popular, the Guess Who has sold 25-million records in two years. Members of the group came together in Winnipeg around 1958, but the present name dates from 1965. Currently, the members, all in their late twenties, are Gary Peterson, Jim Kale, Burton Cummings, Kurt Winter, and Greig Leskiew.

Share the Land

Burton Cummings
Guess Who, **Share the Land**, RCA Victor LSP 4359.
Reprinted by permission of Cirrus Music,
131 Hazelton Avenue, Toronto, Canada.

Have you been around
Have you done your share of comin' down
On different things that people do
Have you been aware
You got brothers and sisters who care
About what's gonna happen to you
In a year from now . . .

> *Refrain:*
> Maybe I'll be there to shake your hand
> Maybe I'll be there to share the land
> That they'll be giving away
> When we all live together.
> We're talkin' 'bout together now. . .

Did you pay your dues
Did you read the news
This morning when the paper landed in your yard
Do you know their names
Can you play their games
Without losing track
And coming down a bit too hard . . .

> *Refrain*

Shake your hand, share the land
Shake your hand, share the land . . .

Nails

Craig Paterson
Sardis Jr/Sr. Secondary School
Vancouver, British Columbia

Jimmy come in!
  take that splinter from your eye,
how did it get there?
  shimmying up a cross
to find some nails for my tree house.

the man there told me to get the hell out
      and away.
  those were his nails
    and no one was to treat lightly
      anything that was his.
i told him that they were rusty and
          no good to him.
he said that they enhance the illuminations.
    he gave in a little though.
        he said that i could have the nails
          of the guy next to him
they aren't doing him any good.

Freedom

Archibald Lampman

Out of the heart of the city begotten
Of the labour of men and their manifold hands,
Whose souls, that were sprung from the earth in her morning,
No longer regard or remember her warning,
Whose hearts in the furnace of care have forgotten
For ever the scent and the hue of her lands;

Out of the heat of the usurer's hold,
From the horrible crash of the strong man's feet;
Out of the shadow where pity is dying;
Out of the clamour where beauty is lying,
Dead in the depth of the struggle for gold;
Out of the din and the glare of the street;

Into the arms of our mother we come,
Our broad strong mother, the innocent earth,
Mother of all things beautiful, blameless,
Mother of hopes that her strength makes tameless,
Where the voices of grief and of battle are dumb,
And the whole world laughs with the light of her mirth.

Over the fields, where the cool winds sweep,
Black with the mould and brown with the loam,
Where the thin green spears of the wheat are appearing,
And the high-ho shouts from the smoky clearing;
Over the widths where the cloud shadows creep;
Over the fields and the fallows we come;

Over the swamps with their pensive noises,
Where the burnished cup of the marigold gleams;
Skirting the reeds, where the quick winds shiver
On the swelling breast of the dimpled river,
And the blue of the kingfisher hangs and poises,
Watching a spot by the edge of the streams;

By the miles of the fences warped and dyed
With the white-hot noons and their withering fires.
Where the rough bees trample the creamy bosoms
Of the hanging tufts of the elder blossoms,
And the spiders weave, and the grey snakes hide,
In the crannied gloom of the stones and the briers;

Over the meadow lands sprouting with thistle,
Where the humming wings on the blackbirds pass,
Where the hollows are banked with the violets flowering,
And the long-limbed pendulous elms are towering,
Where the robins are loud with their voluble whistle,
And the ground-sparrow scurries away through the grass,

Where the restless bobolink loiters and woos
Down in the hollows and over the swells,
Dropping in and out of the shadows,
Sprinkling his music about the meadows,
Whistles and little checks and coos,
And the tinkle of glassy bells;

Into the dim woods full of the tombs
Of the dead trees soft in their sepulchres,
Where the pensive throats of the shy birds hidden,
Pipe to us strangely entering unbidden,
And tenderly still in the tremulous glooms
The trilliums scatter their white-winged stars;

Up to the hills where our tired hearts rest,
Loosen, and halt, and regather their dreams;
Up to the hills, where the winds restore us,
Clearing our eyes to the beauty before us,
Earth with the glory of life on her breast,
Earth with the gleam of her cities and streams.

Here we shall commune with her and no other;
Care and the battle of life shall cease;
Men, her degenerate children, behind us,
Only the might of her beauty shall bind us,
Full of rest, as we gaze on the face of our mother,
Earth in the health and the strength of her peace.

Hand Me Down World

Kurt Winter
Guess Who, **Share the Land**, RCA Victor LSP 4359.
Reprinted by permission of Sunspot Music,
131 Hazelton Avenue, Toronto, Canada.

Anybody here see the noise, see the fear
And commotion,
I think we missed it
Anybody here see the love, see the hate
Being motioned . . .

> *Refrain:*
> Don't give me no hand me down shoes
> Don't give me no hand me down love
> Don't give me no hand me down world
> Got one already.

Anybody here see the long distance cheer
For the notion,
I think we missed it
Anybody here see the sky weeping tears
For the ocean . . .

> *Refrain*

● ● ●

Anybody here see the fuzzy-wuzzy
lovin' cup explosion,
I think we missed it
Anybody here see changing of
the year-end emotion . . .

> *Refrain*

Don't give me no hand me down world
I don't really need it and I'm not gonna take it . . .

I've Tasted my Blood

Milton Acorn

If this brain's over-tempered
consider that the fire was want
and the hammers were fists.
I've tasted my blood too much
to love what I was born to.

But my mother's look
was a field of brown oats, soft-bearded;
her voice rain and air rich with lilacs:
and I loved her too much to like
how she dragged her days like a sled over gravel.

Playmates? I remember where their skulls roll!
One died hungry, gnawing grey perch-planks;
one fell, and landed so hard he splashed;
and many and many
come up atom by atom
in the worm-casts of Europe.

My deep prayer a curse.
My deep prayer the promise that this won't be.
My deep prayer my cunning,
my love, my anger,
and often even my forgiveness
that this won't be and be.
I've tasted my blood too much
to abide what I was born to.

Life is so Strange

Joanne Fillmore
Nova Scotia Teachers College

Life is so strange. . . .
It starts out great,
You have parents
And a sister.
And you feel loved and wanted and secure.
And then your mother's dead . . .
Gone.
And your father can't help
He might as well be gone.
So there's just you and your sister.
And they put you in a home.
You begin to feel secure again
But then they start to ask about the money,
Board money that your father isn't paying.
He says he can't afford to pay
But he drinks.
And so they put you in a new home
And you wonder will you stay.
But you don't.
It's the same old problem
There isn't any money coming in
    for your room and board.
And you shift again.
And you know you won't stay.
Because you never stayed before.
Because there won't be any money.
And after all, who can "support two kids
    who don't even belong to us without
    any money."
So it's a new place.

Home becomes four walls
    for as long as the people will let you stay.
You wonder about things . . .
Things people call home
Security
Love.
But you drift along.
Accepting what comes your way
What foster parents grudgingly hand out.
But you wonder why they can't
    be nice to you.
Why they even took you
    since they don't like you.
And you say to yourself
I didn't ask to be here
You didn't even ask to be born.
But you were born.
You're here.
So you make the best of things.
Things will get better.
Sure.
After all, you do have your sister.
And you're very close to her.
So you're not alone.
You have her
And she has you.
But finally your sister can't take anymore.
She runs away.
And she says, "Hang on, Sis,
    I'll come back for you."
"I'll get you away."

So you wait.
You have faith in her.
But she doesn't come back.
Finally she writes.
She's married.
There's a baby coming.
She misses you and will you write her?
But you're not allowed.
But you write her anyway.
And she sends her answers to school.
And so you slide along
    through the rest of your high school years.
Writing now and then.
But she's changed
It's a whole new world for her.
She has friends
Love
Security
Her husband.
Her baby.
She doesn't need her sister anymore.
But her sister needs her.
But she says, "You won't always be there.
Things will change for you too."
And so you finally do leave.
You go to college.
Life is suddenly wonderful.
You're free.

You feel great.
And you feel secure.
But something happens.
And suddenly
    you're right back to old times.
And those old feelings
Of loneliness
And uncertainty
And unhappiness.
And it's back to those empty,
    crying hours at night.
Because everything is so wrong.
Just being free hasn't changed anything.
There are decisions to make.
And you make the wrong ones
You make so many mistakes
You can't cope with things.
You lose trust and faith.
And your sister isn't writing you at all.
But you do have friends
And they help you.
But you realize people aren't so great.
And life isn't so wonderful.
And no one takes the time to understand
As you thought they would.
And it seems that life is just trying
    to find enough money
    for your room and board.

Bus Rider

Kurt Winter
Guess Who, **Share the land**, RCA Victor LSP 4359.
Reprinted by permission of Sunspot Music,
131 Hazelton Avenue, Toronto, Canada.

Get up in the mornin', get on the bus
Get up in the mornin' like the rest of us
Places to go, important people to meet
Better not get up or you might lose your seat
Bus rider

Leave the house at six o'clock to be on time
Leave the wife and kids at home to make a dime
Grab your lunch pail check for mail in your slot
You won't get your cheque if you don't punch the clock
Bus rider

Grab the evenin' paper and sit down in your chair
Grab yourself a toupée, cause you're losin' your hair
Doesn't matter what you do you've nothin' to lose
I'm so awful goddamn glad I'm not in your shoes
Bus rider . . .

The Lifeless Wife

Margaret Atwood

The lifeless wife
Kisses with pursed lips
Her grim husband (thin
Pinstriped businessman);
She is his safe
Deposit box and bank,
The nickelodeon
That plays his favourite tune.

She was just an ordinary
Woman: all he had to do
To make her fully his
In pure domestic bliss
Was just break through
Her backbone, empty out her head,
Stuff her heart with money
And bury her in bed.

The Prodigal Son

Gilles Hénault
translated by F. R. Scott

The child who used to play see him now thin and bowed
The child who used to weep see now his burned-out eyes
The child who danced a round see him running after a streetcar
The child who longed for the moon see him satisfied with a mouthful of bread
The wild and rebellious child, the child at the end of the town
In the remote streets
The child of adventures
Of the ice of the river
The child perched on fences
See him now in the narrow road of his daily routine
The child free and lightly clothed, see him now
Disguised as a bill-board, a sandwich-man
Dressed up in cardboard laws, a prisoner of petty taboos
Subdued and trussed, see him hunted in the name of justice
The child of lovely red blood and of good blood
See him now the ghost of a tragic opera

The prodigal son
The child prodigy, look at him now as a man
The man of 'time is money' and the man of *bel canto*
The man riveted to his work which is to rivet all day

The man of the Sunday afternoons in slippers
And the interminable bridge parties
The numberless man of the sports of the few men
And the man of the small bank account
To pay for the burial of a childhood that died
Towards its fifteenth year

For P. H. E.

Pat Ellis
Mission Senior Secondary School
Mission City, British Columbia

I can see you as a cowboy,
Riding the dusty horses
In second-rate rodeos
And getting drunk at cheap bars
Or smoking rough, home-cured,
Brush-grown weed in a shabby bunkhouse.

Who would have thought you to be
A volleyball player
And Mathematics enthusiast,
Or an architect, caged in his creativity
Of planning dwellings and office buildings?

I would have preferred to find you
Lying back in the sun-sprung forest
With a double-headed axe at your feet,
Tossing your shaggy head back
To receive the glittery tan froth
Of Uncle Ben's finest
In your thin-lipped mouth.

I would have liked to have been
Your secret lady,
Waiting tables in a dingy cafe
By the highway,
My hair sleazily pinned back,
Thinking of what time
Will you be home.

I'd let down my tattery masses of hair
And comb it till it was soft and glossy,
Then shed my food-scented clothing
And carefully bathe and perfume
My work-shaken body.

Oh, to greet you
In the chill of crisp sheets
And heavy blankets,
Your soft, chuckling voice
Catching on your lisp
As you tell me,
Between aggressive kisses,
How many trees you felled today.

Maybe you'd be laughter-tickled
To read this now,
But I still don't want for you
The endless closures
And suffocations
Of an office in some skyscraper
Or a sun-sticky studio
In Langley or Ladner.

I'd rather know
That you are a part of the land,
Wordlessly laughing at the salt sea
On a tramp tugboat,
Or chasing chocolate and ebony cattle
Over sun-tanned Cariboo highlands
On a tough, picture-book buckskin mare.

Stompin' Tom Connors

6

Many academics may be shocked to find Stompin' Tom
Connors and Robert W. Service in this anthology of Canadian
poetry. For them, poetry is far too pure and exalted a thing
to be expressed by mere working men. Beware of these people.
Anyone who cannot respond to the warmth, vigour, and joy
in life that Connors and Service capture so well in their rough
songs of the common man, will probably also be dead to much
that is in Shakespeare and Chaucer.

Service has long been famous as a worker's poet. Only recently,
however, has Tom Connors emerged as the leading worker's
troubadour. Born in St. John, New Brunswick in 1937, Connors
was adopted by foster parents in Prince Edward Island, ran
away to Halifax when he was thirteen, and then spent a decade
wandering as a vagabond and labourer all over Canada, con-
stantly writing and singing songs about the jobs he'd had and
the people he'd met. His big break came in Timmins, Ontario,
in 1964, when he actually got paid for singing. He is now
Canada's top country singer, with ten albums to his name
and a heap of half-inch plywood boards he's broken to bits
while "stompin'" out his songs. For all the people who don't
count, and should, Stompin' Tom Connors is Canada's Woody
Guthrie.

In contrast to the robust works of Connors and Service, "Hard
Times", a traditional Eskimo poem, and "Waterfront", by
sixteen-year-old Cass Longard of Nova Scotia, show how poets
can also invest the life of working people with beauty and
dignity.

Sudbury Saturday Night

Tom Connors
Tom Connors, **Stompin' Tom Connors Meets Big Joe Mufferaw**, Dominion LPS 21007.
Copyright Crown-Vetch Music Ltd. (CAPAC). Used by permission.

Refrain:
The girls are out to Bingo and the boys are gettin' stinko,
We think no more of I.N.C.O. on a Sudbury Saturday Night.
The glasses they will tinkle when our eyes begin to twinkle
And we think no more of I.N.C.O. on a Sudbury Saturday Night.

With Irish Jim O'Connell there and Scotty Jack MacDonald
There's honky Fred'rick Hurgel gettin' tight, but that's all right.
There's happy German Fritzy there with Frenchy gettin' tipsy
And even Joe the Gypsy knows it's Saturday tonight.

Now when Mary, Ann and Mabel come to join us at the table
And tell us how the Bingo went tonight, we'll look a fright,
But if they won the money we'll be lappin' up the honey, boys,
'Cause everything is funny for it's Saturday tonight.

Refrain

We'll drink the loot we borrowed and recuperate tomorrow
'Cause everything is wonderful tonight, we had a good fight,
We ate the Dilly Pickle and we forgot about the Nickel
And everybody's tickled for it's Saturday tonight.

The songs that we'll be singin', they might be wrong but they'll be ringin'
When all the lights of town are shinin' bright and we're all tight,
We'll get to work on Monday but tomorrow's only Sunday
And we're out to have a fun-day for it's Saturday tonight.

Refrain

Hard Times

Traditional Eskimo Poem

Hard times, dearth times
Plague us every one,
Stomachs are shrunken,
Dishes are empty. . . .

Mark you there yonder?
There come the men
Dragging beautiful seals
To our homes.
Now is abundance
With us once more,
Days of feasting
To hold us together.
Know you the smell
Of pots on the boil?
And lumps of blubber
Slapped down by the side bench?
Joyfully
Greet we those
Who brought us plenty!

Waterfront

Cass Longard
Sir John A. MacDonald High School
Halifax County, Nova Scotia

The wind wheezing rough and cold,
Scraping the skin off cheeks,
Picks up the sea and beats it
Against the shore,
While duffle-bagged men,
Who shadow the waterfront,
Swagger within the
Rhythm of the sea
Along salt-slimed decks.
And ships with hulls embroidered
With french-knot barnacles
And with straw masts
Spider slung with
Oil-slicked hemp web
Wallow, hog-tied to docks,
Straining, like foaling mares
Shying at their bits. Then,
Outgoing fleets carrying
Vulture picked carrion upon
Their brawny shoulders clamber
Up and over the swells lifting
And lugging the ocean floor
Across the Atlantic to be
Dragged up on foreign shores.

The Spell of the Yukon

Robert W. Service

I wanted the gold, and I sought it;
    I scrabbled and mucked like a slave.
Was it famine or scurvy—I fought it;
    I hurled my youth into a grave.
I wanted the gold and I got it—
    Came out with a fortune last fall,—
Yet somehow life's not what I thought it,
    And somehow the gold isn't all.

No! There's the land. (Have you seen it?)
    It's the cussedest land that I know,
From the big, dizzy mountains that screen it,
    To the deep, deathlike valleys below.
Some say God was tired when He made it;
    Some say it's a fine land to shun;
Maybe: but there's some as would trade it
    For no land on earth—and I'm one.

You come to get rich (damned good reason),
    You feel like an exile at first;
You hate it like hell for a season,
    And then you are worse than the worst.
It grips you like some kinds of sinning;
    It twists you from foe to a friend;
It seems it's been since the beginning;
    It seems it will be to the end.

I've stood in some mighty-mouthed hollow
    That's plumb-full of hush to the brim;
I've watched the big, husky sun wallow
    In crimson and gold, and grow dim,
Till the moon set the pearly peaks gleaming,
    And the stars tumbled out, neck and crop;
And I've thought that I surely was dreaming,
    With the peace o' the world piled on top.

The summer—no sweeter was ever;
    The sunshiny woods all athrill;
The greyling aleap in the river,
    The bighorn asleep on the hill.
The strong life that never knows harness;
    The wilds where the caribou call;
The freshness, the freedom, the farness—
    O God! how I'm stuck on it all.

The winter! the brightness that blinds you,
    The white land locked tight as a drum,
The cold fear that follows and finds you,
    The silence that bludgeons you dumb.
The snows that are older than history,
    The woods where the weird shadows slant;
The stillness, the moonlight, the mystery,
    I've bade 'em goodbye—but I can't.

There's a land where the mountains are nameless,
     And the rivers all run God knows where;
There are lives that are erring and aimless,
     And deaths that just hang by a hair;
There are hardships that nobody reckons;
     There are valleys unpeopled and still;
There's a land—oh, it beckons and beckons,
     And I want to go back—and I will.

They're making my money diminish;
     I'm sick of the taste of champagne.
Thank God! when I'm skinned to a finish
     I'll pike to the Yukon again.
I'll fight—and you bet it's no sham-fight;
     It's hell!—but I've been there before;
And it's better than this by a damsite—
     So me for the Yukon once more.

There's gold, and it's haunting and haunting;
     It's luring me on as of old;
Yet it isn't the gold that I'm wanting,
     So much as just finding the gold.
It's the great, big, broad land 'way up yonder,
     It's the forests where silence has lease;
It's the beauty that thrills me with wonder,
     It's the stillness that fills me with peace.

Lighthouse

7

The Guess Who, The Band, and Lighthouse are the "big three" of Canadian rock. Others may be louder, but these groups use volume only as one dimension of often highly subtle musical and lyric productions, displaying the peculiar Canadian genius for varying restraint and sincerity in a rich variety of moods. At its best, British rock poetry is characterized by fine irony while good American rock lyrics tend to range from simple sincerity to passionate outcries. Distinctively Canadian work, however, moves between these extremes, qualified by the reflective feeling so characteristic of Canadian song-poets like Cockburn, Mitchell, and Cohen. Typical examples are the Lighthouse's driving yet gently whimsical songs, "Mr. Candleman" and "One Fine Morning". The poems conjoined with them further evidence this gift of fancy that our Canadian winters and isolations have never managed to take away from us.

Lighthouse was organized in the late sixties by Skip Prokop, a Canadian whose talent as a drummer has earned him a high reputation among rock musicians in both Britain and North America. The group is now an eleven piece band combining orchestral and rock instruments.

Mr. Candleman

Skip Prokop
Paul Hoffert
Lighthouse, **Peacing It All Together,** Victor LSP 4325.

Jack o' Lantern woke up one day
And his light had disappeared
Who could he call on, what could he do
It was the only thing that he feared
So he ran downstairs to the Superintendent
To catch him before it was five
And the little old man in the engineer's coat
Was asleep beside the power line.

"Hey, Mister Candleman, light my life again
Hey, Mister Candleman, wanna feel your flame within
That's all I want."

Jack o' Lantern said, "I'm not uptight
But I'm no good if I can't be
Shining brightly in the darkened halls
Just to help the workers see
Where they're going
So they don't trip on the things left lying around."
But the little old man in the engineer's coat
Was asleep, he didn't hear a sound.

"Hey, Mister Candleman, light my life again
Hey, Mister Candleman, wanna feel your flame within . . .
Me, oh yeah!"

Jack o' Lantern climbed on a chair
To whisper in the old man's ear
"Please, Mr. Superintendent
Without some help I'll disappear."
Well, the old man laughed 'cause Jack didn't know
It was a game he always played
And he said, "Jack o' Lantern, if you want to shine
'Please' is all you have to say."

"Please, Mister Candleman, light my life again
Please, Mister Candleman, wanna feel your flame w
Me, oh yeah!
OH YEAH!"

The Sorcerer

A. J. M. Smith

There is a sorcerer in Lachine
Who for a small fee will put a spell
On my beloved, who has sea green
Eyes, and on my doting self as well.

He will transform us, if we like, to goldfish:
We shall swim in a crystal bowl,
And the bright water will go swish
Over our naked bodies; we shall have no soul.

In the morning the syrupy sunshine
Will dance on our tails and fins.
I shall have her then all for mine,
And Father Lebeau will hear no more of her sins.

Come along, good sir, change us into goldfish.
I would put away intellect and lust,
Be but a red gleam in a crystal dish,
But kin of the trembling ocean, not of the dust.

Elijah

A. M. Klein

Elijah in a long beard
With a little staff
Hobbles through the market
And makes the children laugh.

He crows like a rooster,
He dances like a bear,
While the long-faced rabbis
Drop their jaws to stare.

He tosses his skullcap
To urchin and tot,
And catches it neatly
Right on his bald spot.

And he can tell stories
Of lovers who elope;
And terrible adventures
With cardinal and pope.

Without a single pinch, and
Without a blow or cuff,
We learned from him the Aleph,
We learned from him the Tauph.

Between the benedictions
We would play leapfrog—
O, this was a wonderful
Synagogue!

He can make a whistle
From a gander's quill;
He can make a mountain
Out of a molehill.

Oh, he is a great man!
Wished he, he could whoop
The moon down from heaven,
And roll it like a hoop;

Wished he, he could gather
The stars from the skies,
And juggle them like marbles
Before our very eyes.

Flight of the Roller-Coaster

Raymond Souster

Once more around should do it, the man confided . . .

And sure enough, when the roller-coaster reached the peak
Of the giant curve above me, screech of its wheels
Almost drowned by the shriller cries of the riders—

Instead of the dip and plunge with its landslide of screams
It rose in the air like a movieland magic carpet, some wonderful bird,

And without fuss or fanfare swooped slowly across the amusement park,
Over Spook's Castle, ice-cream booths, shooting-gallery; and losing no height

Made the last yards above the beach, where the cucumber-cool
Brakeman in the last seat saluted
A lady about to change from her bathing-suit.

Then, as many witnesses duly reported, headed leisurely over the water,
Disappearing mysteriously all too soon behind a low-lying flight of clouds.

One Fine Morning

Skip Prokop
Keith Jolimore
Lighthouse, **One Fine Morning**, GRT 9320-1002
Copyright C.A.M.-U.S.A. Inc. Used by permission.

One fine morning, girl, I'll wake up
Wipe the sleep from my eyes
Go outside and feel the sunshine
Then I know I'll realize
That as long as you love me, girl, we'll fly

And on that morning when I wake up
See your face inside a cloud
See you smile inside a window
Hear your voice inside a crowd
Calling, "Come with me baby, and we'll fly"

    Refrain:
    Yeah we'll fly
    Yeah we'll fly
    We'll fly
    Yeah we'll fly

And on that morning when I wake up
We'll go outside and live our dreams
Our bodies candies made of stardust
And little dolls dressed up in moonbeams
And everywhere we go we'll laugh and sing
I'll kiss you morning, noon and night
And all the universe will smile on us
'Cause they'll know that our love is finally right

    Refrain

Yeah we'll fly to the east
We'll fly to the west
There's no place we can't call our own
Yeah we'll fly to the north
We'll fly to the south
Every planet will become our own
All right!

Poem

Louise Dolen
Westbrook School
Cochrane, Alberta

Back in the forest
to lose myself and find myself
and fall back dying once more

It is the first morning of our love
our sighs are all snow—silver white
and clean as table napkins

The day gone or going
we'll bus from room to room
and I'll protest the eyes of furniture
or flowers
or anything that looks at you but me.

Touchstone

Stuart Holtby
Nepean High School
Ottawa, Ontario

I have lived
that I have cut her seething blue
to diamonds with my hull,
flew full and screaming down
half-drowned from pounding crests
                              to nothing but
the next white fight ahead
my arms half-dead from steering blind
beneath the roar that binds my heart
            to hers
            and stirs it with her every breath.

Birdless Skies

Eve Nagy
St. Martin de Porres Junior High School
Calgary, Alberta

Something should be said for birds
that venture into birdless skies
while wistful birds . . .
hypochondriacs and cripples
creep over the ground
having seen storms and believing
that clouds
are traps for the trusting.

Beverly Glenn-Copeland

8

Recently, the walls between popular and "serious" music have been breeched on yet another side by the extraordinary Beverly Glenn-Copeland, a performer whose voice moves so easily between classical and pop-style singing that it is frequently impossible to distinguish the difference. Furthermore, her music and lyrics reinforce this ease of movement, the result being a true fusion of art song and popular ballad. Joni Mitchell and Leonard Cohen have already gone far toward achieving this fusion, but their liberating of the popular song was mainly a freeing of its lyrics; Beverly Glenn-Copeland has now freed the music.

To appreciate what she is doing, one should compare her recording of " Colour of Anyhow" and "Erzili" with some of the art songs of Schubert. It is especially important to hear how her singing transforms the lyrics of "Erzili" into an encounter with mystic experience, an encounter echoed in the accompanying poems of Pat Lane and Gwendolyn MacEwen.

Colour of Anyhow

Beverly Glenn-Copeland
Beverly Glenn-Copeland, GRT 9233-1001.
Copyright 1971 Overlea Music Limited.

Look into my eyes
The colour of anyhow
Their season needs you now, anyway
And I won't ask you when you're leavin'
Or how long you're plannin' to stay.

Look into my eyes
The country of anywhere
The roads will take you there, anytime
And I won't ask how long you'll love me
Babe, though it's on my mind.

Look into my eyes
Forever the paling hour
That reveals your power and your fears
And I won't ask what was gained babe
Between your lovin' and your tears.

Love poem

Miriam Waddington

I will swallow your
eyes and leave only
pools of darkness.

I will take the words
from your mouth and leave
only lakes of stillness.

Attend to my miracle,
I am kissing your body
making it white as stone,

The pools and lakes
of your eyes and mouth,
the white stone

Of your body will
make a labyrinth
of fabled cities,

And a marbled palace
of many rooms where
the whole world

Will be glad to pay
admission to wander
through the many rooms,

To look at my
miracle pools and soft
monuments until

At last the whole world
will go to sleep happy
at eight o'clock

Under a soft white fleece.

Sonnet
from By Stubborn Stars

Kenneth Leslie

The silver herring throbbed thick in my seine,
silver of life, life's silver sheen of glory;
my hands, cut with the cold, hurt with the pain
of hauling the net, pulled the heavy dory,
heavy with life, low in the water, deep
plunged to the gunwale's lips in the stress of rowing,
the pulse of rowing that puts the world to sleep,
world within world endlessly ebbing, flowing.
At length you stood on the landing and you cried,
with quick low cries you timed me stroke on stroke
as I steadily won my way with the fulling tide
and crossed the threshold where the last wave broke
and coasted over the step of water and threw
straight through the air my mooring line to you.

If You Can Tell Me

Sandra Abma
Garson-Falconbridge School
Garson, Ontario

if you
can tell me
why he left
i'll give you a shining ribbon
to tie
    or throw
        away
    just tell me,

a shining ribbon
    would look
        so pretty
in your hair,

I don't cry
    so don't worry
tell me,
    it would make me
    so happy
    to have the truth
      and
    to see a ribbon
    in your hair.

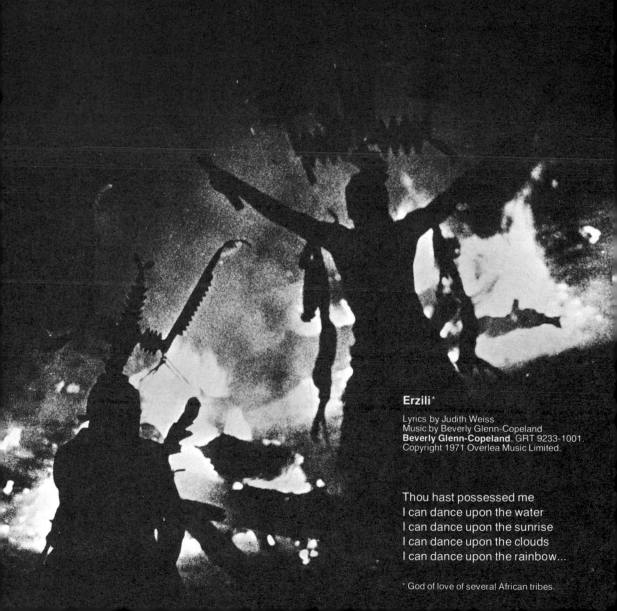

Erzili*

Lyrics by Judith Weiss
Music by Beverly Glenn-Copeland
Beverly Glenn-Copeland. GRT 9233-1001.
Copyright 1971 Overlea Music Limited.

Thou hast possessed me
I can dance upon the water
I can dance upon the sunrise
I can dance upon the clouds
I can dance upon the rainbow...

* God of love of several African tribes.

The Black Colt

Pat Lane

All day light stuttered
as the slow uncertain hills
were captured by dark clouds
rolling out of the Monashee.
It was when the sky split
that the black colt screamed,
eyes rolling,
tail stretched stiff in the wind.

He smelled it coming.
The charred air and her sweat.
Early in the day he tethered her,
drove a peg in deep, leaving her
earth-bound in the pasture
When the storm struck, she braced
and screamed,
heaved on the leather rope.

Between them now is a madness.

Today with mountains firm
under a silent sky he approached her
with soft singing and sweet oats
but she ran to her tether's end,
driving to break the binding.

But the peg he buried is deep.

Soon enough she'll come
choking with hunger, weak,
the madness gone with the god
who came to her in her last wildness.

Manzini: Escape Artist

Gwendolyn MacEwen

now there are no bonds except the flesh; listen—
there was this boy, Manzini, stubborn with
gut stood with black tights and a turquoise
leaf across his sex

and smirking while the big
brute tied his neck arms legs, Manzini
naked waist up and white with sweat

struggled. Silent, delinquent, he
was suddenly all teeth and knee, straining slack
and excellent with sweat, inwardly

wondering if Houdini would take as long
as he; fighting time and the drenched
muscular ropes, as though his tendons were worn
on the outside—

as though his own guts were the ropes
encircling him; it was beautiful; it was thursday; listen—
there was this boy, Manzini

finally free, slid as snake from
his own sweet agonized skin, to throw his entrails
white upon the floor
with a cry of victory—

now there are no bonds except the flesh,
but listen, it was thursday, there was this boy,
Manzini—

Murray McLauchlan

9

Security or *freedom?* In the West, that has been a key issue,
for the history of individuals as well as of nations. The Youth
Revolt of the sixties gave this question a special personal significance for millions of young people in affluent North American
society. In "Child's Song", Murray McLauchlan lets us feel
the price they pay in breaking away from the warmth and comfort of home in order to find themselves according to their
own special visions. But McLauchlan can also celebrate the
fun of taking such an adventure, as in his delightfully irreverent,
"Jesus, Please Don't Save Me Till I Die".

Born in Scotland in 1948, McLauchlan grew up in North Toronto,
graduated from art school, and left home with 35 cents in
his pocket. Logger, fruit picker, and sawmill worker, he spent
his early years wandering over the country. He says, "It was
great—like being on Mars". For him "the whole point of music
is to have a party".* The response to his first album issued
this year indicates that his party is becoming nation-wide.

*See *Grapevine,*
December 23,
1971, p. 26.

The Child's Song

Murray McLauchlan
Murray McLauchlan, **Song from the Street,** True North (Columbia) TN 4.
Copyright 1970 OYSTER MUSIC, 75 East 55th St. N.Y., N.Y. 10022. Used by permission.

Goodbye, Mama, goodbye to you too, Pa
Little sister, you'll have to wait a while to come along
Goodbye to this house and all its mem'ries
We all just got too old to say we're wrong
I've got to make one last trip to my bedroom
I guess I'll have to leave some stuff behind
It's funny how the same old crooked pictures
Just don't look the same to me tonight.

There ain't no use in shedding no more tears, Ma
And there ain't no use in shouting at me, Pa
I can't live no longer with your fears, Ma
I love you but that hasn't helped at all
All of us has gotta do what matters
And each of us must see what we can see
Though it was long ago you must remember
That you were once as young and scared as me.

Mama, I don't know how hard it is yet
When you realize you're growing old
I know how hard it is now to be younger
And I know you've tried to keep me from the cold
Thanks for all you've done—it may sound hollow
Thank you for the good times that we've known
But I must have my own road to follow
You will all be welcome in my home.

So I have got my suitcase, I must go now,
I don't mind about the things you said
Sorry, Ma, I don't know where I'm going
And remember, little sister, look ahead
Tomorrow I'll be in some other sunrise
Maybe I'll have someone by my side
Mama, give your love back to your husband
Father, you have taught me well, Goodbye.

Goodbye, Mama, goodbye to you too, Pa.

In Season

Phyllis Gotlieb

I watch
      chameleons and
children, children and
chameleons: one
elegant appetite sheds
skin every three weeks or
so, slits
seam on his tooth edge
spine bump grind and
shimmies around till he
stands loosened in the trans
lucent shimmy of his own skin
shoots cuff sloughs grabbing
with claw, gobbles it
down to save protein and swift
flick-switches to try out
the same brown/green he started
with
      children

writhing yearning and striving
hoicked up by jerky inches
measured wristbare and pantsleg
put out rawbone joint sweat gland
sex stirring trying to sow miracles
without seed casing the raw still
power, bust
clothes knee elbow & prat &
jettison ragged shirt, wracked
shoe leavings of outcast
armories
      how pectoral grooves the steel
breastplate shapes of the warm
skin form them
      in season I watch
them outgrow my arms

Father

Dale Zieroth

Twice he took me in his hands and shook
me like a sheaf of wheat, like a dog shakes
a snake, as if he meant to knock out my tongue
and grind it under his heel right there
on the kitchen floor. I never remembered
what he said or the warnings he gave; she
always told me afterwards, when he
had left and I had stopped my crying. I
was eleven that year and for seven more years
I watched his friends laughing and him
with his great hands rising and falling
with every laugh, smashing down on his knees
and making the noise of a tree when it cracks
in winter. Together they drank chokecherry
wine and talked of dead friends and the
old times when they were young and because
I never thought of getting old, their
youth was the first I knew of dying.

Sunday before church he would trim
his fingernails with the hunting knife
his East German cousins had sent, the same
knife he used for castrating pigs and
skinning deer: things that had nothing
to do with Sunday. Communion once
a month, a shave every third day, a
good chew of snuff, these were the things
that helped a man to stand in the sun for
eight hours a day, to sweat through each
cold hail storm without a word, to freeze
fingers and feet to cut winter wood, to do
the work that bent his back a little more
each day down toward the ground.

Last Christmas, for the first time, he
gave presents, unwrapped and bought
with pension money. He drinks mostly coffee
now, sleeping late and shaving everyday.
Even the hands have changed: white, soft,
unused hands. Still he seems content
to be this old, to be sleeping in the middle
of the afternoon with his mouth open as if there
is no further need for secrets, as if he is
no longer afraid to call his children "Fools!"
for finding different answers, different lives.

Keine Lazarovitch 1870-1959

Irving Layton

When I saw my mother's head on the cold pillow,
Her white waterfalling hair in the cheeks' hollows,
I thought, quietly circling my grief, of how
She had loved God but cursed extravagantly his creatures.

For her final mouth was not water but a curse,
A small black hole, a black rent in the universe,
Which damned the green earth, stars and trees in its stillness
And the inescapable lousiness of growing old.

And I record she was comfortless, vituperative,
Ignorant, glad, and much else besides; I believe
She endlessly praised her black eyebrows, their thick weave,
Till plagiarizing Death leaned down and took them for his mould.

And spoiled a dignity I shall not again find,
And the fury of her stubborn limited mind;
Now none will shake her amber beads and call God blind,
Or wear them upon a breast so radiantly.

O fierce she was, mean and unaccommodating;
But I think now of the toss of her gold earrings,
Their proud carnal assertion, and her youngest sings
While all the rivers of her red veins move into the sea.

Before Two Portraits of my Mother

Émile Nelligan
translated by George Johnston

I love the beautiful young girl of this
portrait, my mother, painted years ago
when her forehead was white, and there was no
shadow in the dazzling Venetian glass

of her gaze. But this other likeness shows
the deep trenches across her forehead's white
marble. The rose poem of her youth that
her marriage sang is far behind. Here is

my sadness: I compare these portraits, one
of a joy-radiant brow, the other care-
heavy: sunrise—and the thick coming on

of night. And yet how strange my ways seem,
for when I look at these faded lips my heart
smiles, but at the smiling girl my tears start.

Eden is a Zoo

Margaret Atwood

I keep my parents in a garden
among lumpy trees, green sponges
on popsickle sticks. I give them a lopsided
sun which drops its heat
in spokes the colour of yellow crayon.

They have thick elephant legs,
quills for hair and tiny heads;
they clump about under the trees
dressed in the clothes of thirty years
ago, on them innocent as plain skin.

Are they bewildered when they come across
corners of rooms in the forest,
a tin cup shining like pearl,
a frayed pink blanket, a rusted shovel?

Does it bother them to perform
the same actions over and over,
hands gathering white flowers
by the lake or tracing designs in the sand,
a word repeated till it hangs carved
forever in the blue air?

Are they content?

Do they want to get out?

Do they see me looking at them
from across the hedge of spikes
and cardboard fire painted red
I built with so much time
and pain, but
they don't know is there?

Jesus, Please Don't Save Me

Murray McLauchlan
Murray McLauchlan, **Song from the Street**, True North (Columbia) TN 4.
Copyright 1970 OYSTER MUSIC, 75 East 55th St., N.Y., N.Y. 10022. Used by permission.

When I was a little boy
My mama she did say
A whole lot of terrible things'd happen to me
If I ever did chance to stray,
Well, now I'm a little bit older
And I look back on the things I've done
Of all of the times I've strayed from the road
I'm happy 'bout every one

Refrain:
Jesus, please don't save me till I die
I'll be too old to do anythin' that's bad by and by
I've got no wish to cool it while I still can fly
Jesus, please don't save me till I die

My mama said not to mess with no women
Said she was the only good one I'd ever know
But I found out that she was a-missin' the point
The older I did grow,
This girl walked up and took a look at me
And she gave me a great big smile
For the first time I fell from mama's straight and narrow road
And for the first time I could see for miles

Refrain

Yes and now I'm a little bit older
And I look back on the things I've done
I never have hurt nobody
I never did hurt no one,
No I never have hurt nobody
And that's the way that things are gonna stay
And every night when I say me prayers
Here is what I'm gonna say:

Refrain   87

When I Was Eight

Kenneth Yukich

when i was only eight
and the sunflowers were full from the sun
i told my mother i didn't think there was a god
and she called the priest
and he took me for a ride in his car
and he said there was a god
and gave me a chocolate bar
and i asked him why and why there was a hatred
and a war and could i have another chocolate bar.
he said god doesn't work that way.

they sit confident

Poppy Gemmell

They sit, confident, expectant
Await my plea for mercy:
Explain the sun-tanned dreams
Excuse the vagrant ways.

There are no reasons
There is no answer
No counter-charge
And no defence.

These worn out sandals tell the story
Charred by the stars beneath my feet.

A Blatant Cancer

Maruta Straubergs
Bowness High School
Calgary, Alberta

Write me in a straight line!
Write me in a box!
I will bulge your box until
the edges crack and crumble
like an overripe watermelon
And the straight and narrow place
Gapes like the hole in my mind
where the steady drops have fallen
on the stone and killed it with
their saccharin sweetness and cheap reward
     And then you ask me what is real
But I can't answer you because
the taste in my mouth is bitter
and hateful as life itself
when I cannot breathe your rotting air
and self-righteous mortality
     And though you have writ
You have not imprisoned me because you
Forgot to take away the piece of chalk
I hid in that hole.
     I shall write for you
A line of twisted graffiti on the wall
And dying, breathe at you my
Almond breath and LAUGH!

Perth County Conspiracy

10

For some years now, a number of young Canadians have been building bridges between the new youth culture and the ways and ideals of their ancestors. In and around Perth County, Ontario, they are establishing small family farms, working as artisans, and coming together to share and celebrate their break with modern consumer capitalism and their belief in love, simplicity, and nature. Their totally unstructured movement or "conspiracy" is at once profoundly radical, conservative, and Canadian—and it is still going strong.

The Black Swan Coffee House in Stratford, Ontario, is their gathering place, and the spokesmen of their culture are the poet-musicians Cedric Smith and Richard Keelan, two remarkably gifted performers whose vision of life is spreading quietly but surely among young people all over Canada. The songs included here convey the content and, more importantly, the essential feeling of the Perth County philosophy. Among the poems I have chosen to complement that philosophy, the most significant is Milton Acorn's magnificent "I Shout Love". I deeply regret not having space enough to reprint it in its entirety.

trouble on the farm

Cedric Smith
The Perth County Conspiracy Does Not Exist, Columbia ELS 375.
Reprinted by permission of the author.

well, there's trouble out on the farm when the pigs try to take over
they will confiscate your clover, sometimes even work you over
so always remember who belongs in the sty
the seeds you've been sowing should soon be growing
and flowing towards the light

the scarecrow sits upon the bench his mouth dripping law
well, now it would certainly help if I knew what he was there for
you see, he knows nothing but my name
and I'd rather be judged by the fly buzzin' on the window pane

you've a fear of knowing when you should be glowing
and flowing towards the light . . .

well, life out on the farm is mellow in any weather
we're just floating like a feather running wild together

the seeds you've been sowing should soon be growing
and flowing towards the light

you've a fear of knowing when you should be glowing
and flowing towards the light

State of Siege

Pierre Trottier
translated by F.R. Scott

Fear of the police
Fear of arrests
Made me afraid of permissions
But even more of the unknown
And of the freedom that led to it

Fear of God
Fear of priests
Fear of men
And of the woman who gave them birth

Fear of my sins
Fear of confessing them
Made me afraid to receive grace
And the holiness that came with it

Fear of war
Fear of the enemy
Made me afraid of friends
And of the peace they heralded

Fear of words
Fear of thought
Made me afraid of magic formulas
And of the sorcerers who recited them

Sign of the cross or cry of race
Magic of amulet or mask
Of the fear primitive the Indian fear
Which impelled me to work on the canoe of suicide

I had already carved a paddle of the folksongs
The one that leads up there as high perhaps as the land
Where I might rejoin the Chasse-Galerie

But the minute I was ready
Authority had surrounded me
Had beamed on me its searchlights
Which relentlessly pinned me against the wall
Of the priestless prison of my conscience

Message from the Beholder

Judy Byrne
Belle River District High School
Belle River, Ontario

I belong to the earth
and not the world.
My feet will walk upon soil
not concrete.
The stars will seduce my thoughts
so the glare from neon lights
will not betray my mind.
The words I write will be lyrics
to the gentle breezes
that will not be penetrated by the
cold wind of society
The fires within my heart will
give me comfort
The truth I see will not be a
Distorted reflection of words
told long ago
I will stand alone on this earth
not to be runover by the rushing
crowds.
If you want to reach me
Leave their world
And enter the earth.

For I belong to the earth.

crucifixation cartoon

Richard Keelan
Cedric Smith
The Perth County Conspiracy Does Not Exist, Columbia ELS 375.
Reprinted by permission of the authors.

Refrain:
there's a cross on every tree
when you're learning to be free . . .

when I found her lyin' there
under a blanket of despair
I bent and kissed her troubled brow
and quietly wondered how
a thing like this could come to be

Refrain

and when I speak to her of love
she draws a picture consisting of
the imagery my poetry explores

and when I speak to them of love
they play the music of the dove
on wings of sound I've never flown before

. . . it should come as no surprise
that when I speak to you of love
it's in the air around above your head
it whispers to you from nearly far away
what do you say?

today is the very first day of spring
today we have gathered here to sing
to be in tune with spring's creation
a time for jubilation
to be in tune with life's creation
a time for jubilation

Refrain

it's in the air around above your head
it whispers to you from nearly far away
what do you say?

from I Shout Love

Milton Acorn

I shout Love in a land muttering slack damnation
as I would in a blizzard's blow,
staggering stung by snowfire in the numbing tongues of cold,
for my heart's a furry sharp-toothed thing
that charges out whimpering
even when pain cries the sign written on it.

I shout Love even tho it might deafen you
and never say that Love's a mild thing
for it's hard, a violation
of all laws for the shrinking of people.
I *shout* Love, counting on the hope
that you'll sing and not shatter in Love's vibration.

I shout Love . . . Love . . . It's a net
scooping us weltering, fighting for joy
hearts beating out new tempos against each other.

The wild centre life explodes from a seed
recreates me daily in your eyes' innocence
as a small ancient creature, Love's inventor,
listened to a rainbow of whispers.

I shout Love against the proverbs of the damned
which they pause between clubbings and treacheries
to quote with wise communicative nods . . . I know
they're lies, but know too
that if I declared a truce in this war
they'd turn into pronged truths and disembowel me.

•   •   •

Even I shout Love who aged ten thousand years
before my tenth birthday
in shame, wrath, and wickedness;
shout and grow young as cowards grow old:
Shout Love whom this world's paradoxical joy
makes stammer or keep silent between shoutings,
more held each hour by the wonder of it.

I shout You my Love in a springtime instant
when I wince half pain half joy to notes from an oriole
over balls of frost trapped in quickening roots,
and the tick-tock-tickle of warm rain
trickling into buds'eyes, plucking them open.

I shout Love into your pain when times change and you must change:
minutes seeming final as a judge's sentence
when skies crack and fall
like splinters of mirrors
and gauntle'd fingers, blued as a great rake,
pluck the balled yarn of your brain:

For Love's the spine holding me straight,
the eye in back of my shoulderblades
that sees and beats my heart for all thinkers,
and the touch all over and thru me
I've often called God.

The herring with his sperm makes milk of the wide wrinkling wriggling ocean
where snowy whales jump rolling among whitecaps
as I shout live your Love and the deeds of my words
pollinate the air you're breathing.
Since life's a dream garment hung singing or sighing on a bone tree
why shouldn't it be Love's adventure?

• • •

But what if I came shouting Love now
to you shivering in your blanket
unfed for forty-eight hours?
The liberals goggle over their cocktails
to talk patiently of feeding you,
but I shout Love and I mean business.

I shout Love in those four-letter words
contrived to smudge and put it in a harmless place,
for Love today's a curse and defiance.
Listen you money-plated bastards
puffing to blow back the rolling Earth with your propaganda
        bellows and oh-so-reasoned negations of Creation:
When I shout Love I mean your destruction.

don't you feel fine

Richard Keelan
The Perth County Conspiracy Does Not Exist, Columbia ELS 375.
Reprinted by permission of the author.

do you care to keep your head in motion
close your eyes and open up your ears
who you are is only an illusion
and what you are determined by your fears
who you are is only an illusion
and what you are determined by your fears
know where you go
show yourself the follies of your time

have you known the pleasures of
giving for the sake of getting nothing
loving for the sake of knowing pleasure
knowing for the sake of teaching others
finding ways to spend your hidden treasures

> *Refrain:*
> let yourself go
> let yourself flow
> don't you feel fine . . .

do you want to know what I know
close your mouth and open up your mind
do you want to go where I go
or go ahead and listen to the blind
know what I know
show yourself the follies of your time . . .

> *Refrain*

siddhartha in the south wing

Peter Trower

The blind goal blurs
before the groping eyes
and the fairy tales of youth
are at once behind, beside and beyond us.

The complexion of the effort is grey
and multihued
and we shall reap in the making of it
the well-sown winds of sadness and laughter.

Dark is the journey
and bright as atomspeech . . .
the fable draws us on through the halls of chaos . . .
we are snowballed together in rolling Time . . .
we are the names of our children and the number of wonder . . .
we are the crackle of oblivion and the snarl of simplicity . . .
we are the vocabulary of the volcano. . . .
we are the click of keys turning in phantom locks . . .
we are hope's tempestuousity and the middle name of God . . .
we are the thought behind the thought in the willow . . .
                                        and the willow . . .
we are the conjured dust on the blowing plain of days . . .
we are the grain of sand in the eye of a lost child . . .
we are the poempukers and the poemlivers . . .
we are the lead balloons and the buoyant outerspinners of infinity . . .
we are random arrows from the quiver of the last archer . . .
we are cavepeople looking for the address of Meaning
                                in the yellowstone pages

The Meaning of the I CHING

Eli Mandel

we are the river
and the ripples in the river
and the source and current of the river
and the bedsilt of the river
and the stupidity of the river
and the wisdom of the river
and the joy of the river
and the endless tearflow of the river
and the anxiety of the river
and the peace of the river
and the song of the river
and the omnipresence of the river
and the soul of the river
     and the river
     and the river
     and the river

I

unopened
     book of old men
     orange-blossom book
         before me
you were
     how could you contain me?

do you not see I am the mouths
of telegraphs and cemeteries?
my mother groaned like the whole
of Western Union to deliver
my message
     and yelling birthdays
that unrolled from my lungs
like ticker-tape for presidents
about to be murdered
     I sped
on a line that flew
to the vanishing point of the west

before I was
     you were
unopened book
     do not craze me
with the odour of orange-blossom

do not sit there
like smiling old men

     how could you contain me?

II

under my fingers words form themselves
it's crazy to talk of temples in this day
but light brightens on my page
like today moving against the wooden house
all shapes change and yet stay
as if they were marble in autumn
as if in the marbled yellow autumn
each western house becomes a shrine
stiff against the age of days
under my fingers stiffly formed

one cannot be another, I cry,
let me not be crazed by poetry

I will walk in streets that vanish
noting peculiar elms like old women
who will crash under the storm of sun
that breaks elm, woman, man
into a crumble of stump and bark
until the air is once more clear
in the sane emptiness of fall

III

my body speaks to me
as my arms say: two are one
as my feet say: earth upon earth
as my knees say: bow down, unhinge yourself
as my cells say: we repeat the unrepeatable

the book speaks: arrange yourself in the form
                     that will arrange you

before I was: colours that hurt me
                     arranged themselves in me
before I was: horizons that blind me
                     arranged themselves in me

before I was: the dead who speak to me
                     arranged themselves in me

IV

I am the mouths
of smiling old men

there rises from me
the scent of orange-blossoms

I speak in the words
of the ancient dead

arranged
in the raging sun
in the stiffening age of days

and in the temple of my house

one becomes another
I am crazed by poetry

Joni Mitchell

11

The songs and poems of the last section express the concern of those Canadians who refuse to accept the "Americanization" of their country. Joni Mitchell, whose international fame rests mainly on her reflective, highly personal song-poetry, has also struck some gentle but telling blows against this process, notably in "Big Yellow Taxi", "Woodstock", and the powerful "Fiddle and the Drum". Actually, the boundaries between lyric expression and rhetorical statement are hardly very sharp in these songs. Both elements become artlessly integrated, as is the case with the words and music in all of her best work.

Notice how differently some of Canada's leading poets develop the themes she touches on in these songs. Notice, too, that for them as well as for Joni Mitchell, "Americanization" is not just what the American Establishment is doing to the world; it is rather the symbol of money-centered culture, something that any nation can grow all by itself.

The first song, "Songs to Aging Children," is perhaps more typical of Joni Mitchell's ways of self-revelation. My reason for following it with Eli Mandel's "Marina" is that "Marina" also seems to reveal a Mitchell-like personality, but by means of a very different series of mirrors.

For the record, Joni Mitchell, née Anderson, was born in Fort Macleod, Alberta in 1944, grew up in Saskatoon, Saskatchewan, and in the last three years, has made it to the top of her profession—a place where, perhaps, she would rather not be.

Songs to Aging Children Come

Joni Mitchell
Joni Mitchell, **Clouds**, Reprise RS 6341.
Copyright 1967. Reprinted by permission of the publisher,
Siquomb Publishing Corp.

Through the windless wells of wonder
By the throbbing light machine
In the tealeaf trance or under
Orders from the king and queen

> *Refrain:*
> Songs to aging children come
> Aging children, I am one

People hurry by so quickly
Don't they hear the melodies
In the chiming and the clicking
And the laughing harmonies

> *Refrain*

Some come dark and strange like dying
Crows and ravens whistling
Lines of weeping, strings of crying
So much said in listening

> *Refrain*

Does the moon play only silver
When it strums the galaxy
Dying roses, will they will their
Perfumed rhapsodies to me

> Songs to aging children come
> This is one

Skulls and Drums

Gwendolyn MacEwen

you talked about sound not
footstep sound, shiphorn, nightcry,
                                        but
strings collecting, silver
and catgut, violas riding
the waves of May like soft ships,
                                        yes
and the anchoring senses,
the range, the register,
the index
            in the ear; the long
measure from the drums of our skulls
to the heart (and its particular tempo);
the music anchored there, gathered
in.

you will hear me now, I think,
while my skin still gathers tones of the sun in,
while we ride the bars, the slow passages
of these first minutes;

while the taut drums of our skulls
open
and all sounds enter
and the pores of our skin like slow valves open.

we will hear each other now, I think,
while nothing is known, while sound
and statement in the ear
leave all alternatives;
                            our skulls like drums,
                            like tonal caves
                            echo, enclose.

while the ribs of our bodies are great hulls
and the separate ships of our senses
for a minute

anchor.

for a minute in the same harbour

anchor.

Marina

Eli Mandel

Because she spoke often of the sea we thought she had known
    another country, her people distant, not forgotten

We did not know then who was calling her or what songs she
    listened to or why the sea-birds came to rest
    upon her long fingers

Or why she would shudder like a sea-bird about to take flight,
    her eyes changing with the changing light

As the sea-changing opal changes, as a shell takes its
    colours from the sea as if it were the sea

As if the great sea itself were held in the palm of a hand

They say the daughters of the sea know the language of birds,
    that in their restless eyes the most fortunate learn
    how the moon rises and sets

We do not know who is calling her or why her eyes change
    or what shore she will set her foot upon

Big Yellow Taxi

Joni Mitchell
Joni Mitchell, **Ladies of the Canyon**, Reprise RS 6376.
Copyright 1970. Reprinted by permission of the publisher, Siquomb Publishing Corp.

They paved paradise
Put up a parkin' lot
With a pink hotel, a boutique
And a swingin' hot spot
Don't it always seem to go
That you don't know what you've got
Till it's gone
They paved paradise
Put up a parkin' lot.

They took all the trees
Put them in a tree museum
And they charged the people
A dollar and a half just to see 'em
Don't it always seem to go
That you don't know what you've got
Till it's gone
They paved paradise
Put up a parkin' lot.

Hey farmer farmer
Put away that D.D.T. now
Give me spots on my apples
But leave me the birds and the bees
Please!
Don't it always seem to go
That you don't know what you've got
Till it's gone
They paved paradise
Put up a parkin' lot.

Late last night
I heard the screen door slam
And a big yellow taxi
Took away my old man
Don't it always seem to go
That you don't know what you've got
Till it's gone
They paved paradise
Put up a parkin' lot
I said, don't it always seem to go
That you don't know what you've got
Till it's gone
They paved paradise
Put up a parkin' lot...

Klaxon

James Reaney

All day cars mooed and shrieked,
Hollered and bellowed and wept
Upon the road.
They slid by with bits of fur attached,
Fox-tails and rabbit-legs,
The skulls and horns of deer,
Cars with yellow spectacles
Or motorcycle monocle,
Cars whose gold eyes burnt
With a too-rich battery,
Murderous cars and manslaughter cars,
Chariots from whose foreheads leapt
Silver women of ardent bosom.
Ownerless, passengerless, driverless,
They came to anyone
And with headlights full of tears
Begged for a master,
For someone to drive them
For the familiar chauffeur.
Limousines covered with pink slime
Of children's blood
Turned into the open fields
And fell over into ditches,
The wheels kicking helplessly.
Taxis begged trees to step inside,
Automobiles begged of posts
The whereabouts of their mother.
But no one wished to own them any more,
Everyone wished to walk.

growing up: 1950's

Marc Plourde

we didn't know
why the men came,
we were curious
about their machines

we watched them
tear up our fields,
saw down trees,
pour cement over weeds
and flowers

and we felt cheated
that summer
and summers after that
when nothing ever
grew again

and were told
not to get close
to the new highway

because traffic there
went by so fast
it was just a buzz,
and wind pushing,
and dust in your throat

and because one boy
wandered out
into that place

and a car met him
like the way we used to
crush open an insect
with a stone

The House of the Old Woman

Jeffrey Cuff
Prince of Wales Collegiate
St. John's, Newfoundland

Before you press on,
    enter the parlour.
Anyone may play the old out-of-tune piano
    which rests there.
      The notes are deep and solid—
    everything you play will sound hollow,
    but good.
When you tire of that,
    observe the pictures
    of two small girls,
    Elizabeth and Margaret Rose,
    who stare out of their ovals
    at the boy on the general-store calendar.
Next follow the wooden bannister-rail
    up to the room in which you awoke,
    as the early light
    trickled through the yellow blinds
    and lace curtains.
Remember how you heard the clatter of hooves
    and the lament of sheep and cows
    being driven forward
    by shouting men,
    while faces formed in the wallpaper design.

Or,
    you could walk through the porch door
    with the blue and red glass,
    down the street
    to the new supermarket
    with the regimented rows
    of canned goods.

The Fiddle and the Drum

Joni Mitchell
Joni Mitchell, **Clouds**, Reprise RS 6341.
Copyright 1969. Reprinted by permission of the publisher, Siquomb Publishing Corp.

And so once again
My dear Johnny, my dear friend
And so once again
You are fighting us all
And when I ask you why
You raise your sticks and cry and I fall
Oh, my friend
How did you come
To trade the fiddle for the drum

You say I have turned
Like the enemies you've earned
But I can remember
All the good things you are
And so I ask you please
Can I help you find the peace and the star
Oh, my friend
What time is this
To trade the handshake for the fist

And so once again
Oh America, my friend
And so once again
You are fighting us all
And when we ask you why
You raise your sticks and cry and we fall
Oh, my friend
How did you come
To trade the fiddle for the drum

You say we have turned
Like the enemies you've earned
But we can remember
All the good things you are
And so we ask you please
Can we help you find the peace and the star
Oh, my friend
We have all come
To fear the beating of your drum.

Backdrop addresses cowboy

Margaret Atwood

Starspangled cowboy
sauntering out of the almost-
silly West, on your face
a porcelain grin,
tugging a papier-mâché cactus
on wheels behind you with a string,

you are innocent as a bathtub
full of bullets.

Your righteous eyes, your laconic
trigger-fingers
people the streets with villains:
as you move, the air in front of you
blossoms with targets

and you leave behind you a heroic
trail of desolation:
beer bottles
slaughtered by the side
of the road, bird-
skulls bleaching in the sunset.

I ought to be watching
from behind a cliff or a cardboard storefront
when the shooting starts, hands clasped
in admiration,

but I am elsewhere.

Then what about me

what about the I
confronting you on that border
you are always trying to cross?

I am the horizon
you ride towards, the thing you can never lasso

I am also what surrounds you:
my brain
scattered with your
tincans, bones, empty shells,
the litter of your invasions.

I am the space you desecrate
as you pass through.

Billboards Build Freedom of Choice
(billboard on Oregon coastal highway)

Earle Birney

Yegitit?
Look see
      AMERICA BUILDS BILLBOARDS
so billboards kin bill freedoma choice
between—yeah between billbores no
      WAIT
its yedoan hafta choose no more between
say like trees and billbores lessa course
wenna buncha trees is flattint outtinta
      BILLB—
yeah yegotit
youkin pick between well
hey!   see!   like dat!
      ALL VINYL GET WELL DOLLS $6.98
or—watch wasdat comin up?
      PRE PAID CAT
      PREPAID CATASTROPHE COVERAGE
yeah hell youkin have damnear anythin
      FREE 48 INCH TV IN EVERY ROOM
see!   or   watchit!
      OUR PIES TASTE LIKE MOTHERS
yeah but look bud no chickenin out
because billbores build
      AM—
yeah an AMERICA BUILDS MORE
buildbores to bill more—
sure yugotta! yugotta have
      FREEDOM TO
hey! you doan wannem godam fieldglasses!
theys probly clouds on Mount Raneer

                    but not on
          MOUNT RAINIER THE BEER THAT CHEERS
Landscapes is for the birds fella
yegotta choose between well like
between two a de same
hell like de man said Who's got time
for a third tit? *two* parties is *Okay*
that's   DEMOC   sure but yegit three
yegot COMMIES I'm tellinyeh
is like dose damfool niggers in
in Asia someweres all tryin to be nootrul
I tellyeh treesa crowd   a crowda
godamatheisticunamericananti
          BILLBORES
yeah an yewanna help Burma? help
     BURMA SHAVE
yewanna keep the longhairs from starvin?
          BUY HANDMADE TOY SOLDIERS
yegotta choose fella yegotta
choose between

          AMERICA and UN—

between KEE-RISPIES and KEE-RUMPIES

between KEE-RYEST and KEE ROOST-SHOVE
and brother if you doan pick
     RIGHT
you better
git this heap
tahelloffn
our
          FREEWAY

Oh, Oh, Canada!

Liz Murdoch
Bishop Carroll High School
Calgary, Alberta

i was standing on my maple leaf
holding my beaver
and singing o canada
when i heard a strange sound
a flapping i had heard before
but never this loud
i looked up to behold
a great bald Eagle
Its claws were spread
ready to fight,
Its beak was open
ready to dictate
and then the Eagle squawked,
swooping down toward me.

It took my maple leaf
to help build Its Nest
and It ate my beaver.
i didn't protest much
i figured i'd get something
in return.

i did . . . .

i was standing in the same spot
two days later
and the Eagle flew over
and Eagled on my head.

Woodstock

Joni Mitchell
Joni Mitchell, **Ladies of the Canyon**, Reprise RS 6376.
Copyright 1969. Reprinted by permission of the publisher, Siquomb Publishing Corp.

I came upon a child of God
He was walkin' along the road
And I asked him, where are you goin'
And this he told me
I'm goin' on down to Yasgurs' farm
I'm gonna join in a rock 'n roll band
I'm gonna camp out on the land
I'm gonna try an' get my soul free

Refrain:
We are stardust
We are golden
And we've got to get ourselves
Back to the garden

Then can I walk beside you
I have come here to lose the smog
And I feel to be a cog in somethin' turnin'
Well maybe it is just the time of year
Or maybe it's the time of man
I don't know who I am
But you know life is for learnin'

Refrain

By the time we got to Woodstock
We were half a million strong
And everywhere there was song and celebration
And I dreamed I saw the bombers
Ridin' shotgun in the sky
And they were turnin' into butterflies
Above our nation

We are stardust . . . million year old carbon
We are golden . . . caught in the devil's bargain
And we've got to get ourselves
Back to the garden

Eden

F.R. Scott

Adam stood by a sleeping lion
Feeling its fur with his toes.
He did not hear Eve approaching,
Like a shy fawn she crept close.

The stillness deepened. He turned.
She stood there, too solemn for speech.
He knew that something had happened
Or she never would stay out of reach.

'What is it? What have you found?'
He stared as she held out her hand.
The innocent fruit was shining.
The truth burned like a brand.

'It is good to eat,' she said,
'And pleasant to the eyes,
And—this is the reason I took it—
It is going to make us wise!'

She was like that, the beauty,
Always simple and strong.
She was leading him into trouble
But he could not say she was wrong.

Anyway, what could he do?
She'd already eaten it first.
She could not have all the wisdom.
He'd have to eat and be cursed.

So he ate, and their eyes were opened.
In a flash they knew they were nude.
Their ignorant innocence vanished.
Taste began shaping the crude.

This was no Fall, but Creation,
For although the Terrible Voice
Condemned them to sweat and to labour,
They had conquered the power of choice.

Even God was astonished.
'This man is become one of Us.
If he eat of the Tree of Life . . . !'
Out they went in a rush.

As the Flaming Sword receded
Eve walked a little ahead.
'If we keep on using this knowledge
I think we'll be back,' she said.

Generation Cometh

Gwendolyn MacEwen

the boy
a coy root or
bright among cities
is growing you
cannot stop him you
cannot stop him
growing.

try to
pull him out
by the roots
from your loins he
is green like a tree
planted there

he is in your dark garden
he will eat your dark flowers
you cannot stop him old
men old women you
cannot stop him
growing.

his thumb his
bright brain his
heel is beneath you
send him to school
or macabre churches you
cannot stop him

not even the wild
Muria boy stood
wild and white-toothed
among jungles
and found them
complicated—

he grows beneath your heels
and the city for him is easy he
knows it from below
old men old women you
cannot stop him
growing.

The Metal and the Flower

Dorothy Livesay

Under my windows
the young march and sing
on flute   on zither
on guitar
celebrating autumn
red orange yellow
carrying chrysanthemums
and zinnias
they march into autumn
against the mailed and metalled
study-minded knights
who assail the countryside
ravage the trees the grass
on Vietnam prairies.

The young celebrate once more
innocence and experience
proclaim   in their blue jeans
jackets and long hair
the right to own love
to distribute its blossoms
impervious to all man-
u-factured
metal.

The Band

12

We have spoken of the struggle against "Americanization" waged by Canadian songwriters and poets. There is one kind of Americanization, however, that has been keenly sought after, at least by the song-writers—the attempt to bring the blues and Nashville country music into the mainstream of Canadian popular song.

The people most responsible for integrating the blues and southern country music with Canadian pop are the members of The Band, a group whose importance in international rock almost rivals that of the Rolling Stones and the Beatles. According to *Time*, Jamie "Robbie" Robertson, Rick Dancoe, Richard Mamel, and Garth Hudson, four teenage musicians from Ontario who were total strangers to one another, coincidentally decided about 1960 to go into the deep South in order to learn blues and country "all the way down". Somehow they met, and, returning to Ontario with an American drummer, Levon Helm, formed a group called The Hawks, later to become the back-up for Bob Dylan that created Dylan's famous folk-rock sound in 1965. Now, as The Band, they work at "country rock", a very American sound, qualified, however, by Canadian restraint and lightness. Robertson's "Life is a Carnival" is a good example of their work—on the surface, easy and carefree, but around the edges, buttressed by wry harmonies and a keen awareness of the absurdities of the big show we are all living in.

Life is a Carnival

Rick Danko
Levon Helm
Jamie Robbie Robertson
The Band,**Cahoots**, Capitol SMAS 651.
Copyright 1971. CANAAN MUSIC, INC., 75 E. 55th St., NYC 10022. Used by permission.

You can walk on the water—drown in the sand
You can fly off a mountaintop—if anybody can
Run away—run away—it's the restless age
Look away—look away—you can turn the page

> *Refrain*:
> Hey, Buddy, would you like to buy a watch real cheap
> Here on the street
> I got six on each arm and two more round my feet
> Life is a carnival—believe it or not
> Life is a carnival—two bits a shot

Saw a man with the jinx—in the third degree
From trying to deal with people—people you can't see
Take away—take away—this house of mirrors
Give away—give away—all the souvenirs
We're all in the same boat ready to float off the edge of the world
This flat old world
The street is a sideshow from the peddler to the corner girl
Life is a carnival—it's in the book
Life is a carnival—take another look

> *Refrain*

There's this old vaudeville skit in which a man—
his arms and legs in casts, his torso and head in bandages—
is wheeled onto stage and says sadly,
oh well it beats playing Toronto.

Doug Fetherling

i go 2 strip shows in the afternoon
2 analyze the characterizations in the 4th run
   latvian films w/croation subtitles

         but the girls somehow arouse my poetic interests
         & when i stand up 2 Bravo Bravo
         Miss Nieda Mann as she twirls 1 tassel
            clockwise, the other otherwise
         everybody turns around & stares/

   & when the poor comics' jokes
   are greeted by silence
   i drop a dixie cup or something
   just 2 make some noise

      'When I was 7 years old
      I had a terrible tragedy:
      I lost my mother and father.
      Oh what a crap game that was!'

         & i feel sorry 4 the too skinny dancer
         & the 1 who trips
         & the 1 who cant keep time
         & the 1 who tries 2 twirl her sequined
            bra but winds up winding it up
            around her wrist/

& im out&out bloody heartbroken
when i learn on good authority
that Fifi LaChance La Petite Parisienne
is a plumbing contractor's daughter from calgary

        & im all but clinically insane by the time
        when after the last show
        The Boys In The Band play the national anthem
        & every1
            from the traditional bald headed lecherers
            in the 1st row
            2 the last poor junkie in the rear

                P
               U

             S
             D
           N
          A
        T
       S
        in an attempt 2 make it thru 6 bars of O Canada

    (nationalism has always had a soothing effect on me u see)/

i go 2 strip shows in the afternoon
only 2 stagger out 10 hours later
w/square bags under my eyes
& a sense of having played Toronto///

Pop! Goes the Easel

Phyllis Gotlieb

What happened was
all the fathombeasts that ever bashed
the surface/tension of the
shadowscreen and the silent stealthy shadow
trackers of the killer and the brash ones too the
Bulldog/drummers and Maigret/regretters
Hammers of God/forsaken louts and loonies
King Kongs & Mings of Mongo
came up for air I mean
Pow! right off the page/screen/canvas
alive in simultaneous reality
on this the fairflower of our lambent
earth billboard & boxtop Wow! what
rowwracking nights we had
then, what adrenalin/docked days
running amok the concurrence of walleyed
thieves thugs yeggs mugs spivs till they'd
Docsavaged & Hairsbreadth/harried us, you & me
Bam! onto the page/screen/canvas Greatscott
& Ogeegosh we were

feelin no pain. I mean.
no pain.
no love. Nothing but
flicker & writhe in
2 constrained dimensions no
hailstones gallstones flintstones
were our weather our rage
decalcomania. That's how it crumbled.

Sometimes
they look/read/watch us strange
phenomena of their immaterial
age of ex
crescent dinosaurs & leaping
lizards. And turn away. We stir
no passions, Charley. If they grieve
guiltfingered
Bonds console them. So

kiss me quick before the fade
out and tell me
in one balloon, one frame
                          the way we
played it, what did we have Toulouse
Lautrec?

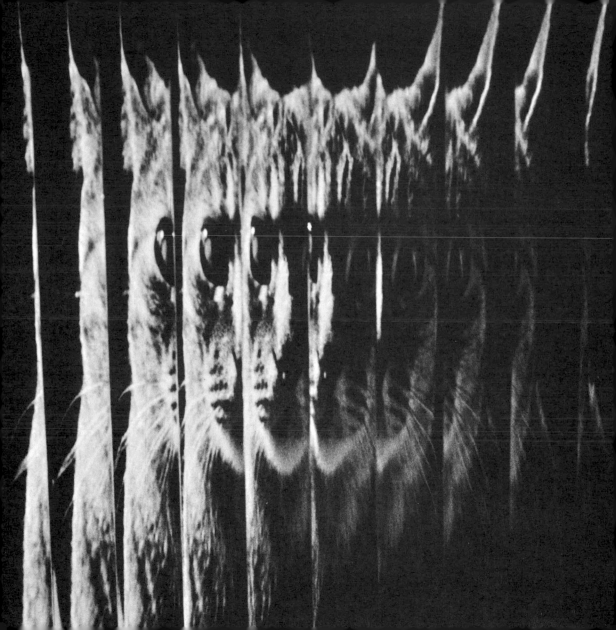

Happy Birthday Kid

Kenneth Yukich

so everyday's not
your birthday kid
and no one is ever around
to light your candles
and you haven't got a penny
or a penny match
and you don't live
in a birthday-cake-house
with candy windows
and chocolate doors
and the enchanted city witch
is only a bitch
who lives next door
and your fairy-godmother
turned out to be a fruit
and when gabriel
blows his horn you're not
going to get up either,
like all the others
you'll be dead
with drying blood bubbles
on your head
so happy birthday.
now get the hell out of here.

Neil Young

13

Loneliness comes in many forms, but perhaps the most profound loneliness comes upon us when we face the mystery surrounding our very existence. Where do we come from? Why are we here? Are we jokes, accidents, or miracles? Most of us try to forget these disturbing questions. There are some, however, who not only insist on facing this mystery, but also give their experience of it in artistic form.

This is the work of Leonard Cohen and Neil Young. Cohen projects the experience of strangeness more magically than any living poet. Young conveys a similar kind of awareness through a special charisma. In songs like "The Loner" and especially "The Last Trip to Tulsa", Young, by means of an almost ethereal voice, driving guitar rhythms, and weird, visionary images, leads us to the edge of madness, and even more remarkably lets us accept it all almost as a matter of fact. The effect in "The Last Trip to Tulsa" is a mixture of black comedy and surrealist humor, a note that is also struck by the contemporary poets Lloyd Abbey, Alden Nowlan, and Michael Ondaatje.

Son of the well-known journalist Scott Young, Neil Young grew up in Winnipeg, quit school after failing grade nine, and tried unsuccessfully to gain recognition as a performer in Canada. Discouraged with Canada, he then went to Los Angeles where he worked with The Buffalo Springfield, Crazy Horse, and the group Crosby, Stills, Nash, and Young. The albums cut by these groups brought him fame and allowed him to become a major solo star. In January, 1971, he returned to Canada for a triumphant concert in Massey Hall, Toronto.

The Loner

Neil Young
Neil Young, Reprise RS 6317.
Copyright 1968 Cotillion Music Inc. &
Broken Arrow Music,
1841 Broadway, N.Y., N.Y., 10023.

he's the perfect stranger
like a cross of himself and a fox
he's a feeling arranger
and a changer of the ways he talks
he's the unforeseen danger
the keeper of the key to the locks

> *Refrain:*
> know when you see him
> nothing can free him
> step aside
> open wide
> it's the loner

if you see him on the subway
he'll be down at the end of the car
watching you move
until he knows who you are
when you get off at your station alone
he'll know that you are

> *Refrain*

there was a woman he knew
about a year or so ago
she had something that he needed
and he pleaded with her not to go
on the day that she left
he died but it did not show

> *Refrain*

There's No Room

Ken Belford

There's no room in the city for wood.
What they want is cement. Permanence,
So they are coming to tear the house down.

Already the caretaker is gone.
Old Stan. The police came, took him away.
Smashed his door in first, not knowing there was no lock.

Went away laughing because they found him cringing
In the corner, clutching the camera he bought
At the department store where he forged the cheque.

I think it was the crone downstairs told me.
The one that paints. But she is not to be believed,
Not caring to sign her name as a witness.

And I wonder where they will go.
The people who stare like animals
At the sun.

Who run the tap water all night long,
Or move the furniture, again, again,
Whispering, whispering in their stale rooms.

Jamie

Elizabeth Brewster

When Jamie was sixteen,
Suddenly he was deaf. There were no songs,
No voices any more.
He walked about stunned by the terrible silence.
Kicking a stick, rapping his knuckles on doors,
He felt a spell of silence all about him,
So loud it made a whirring in his ears.
People moved mouths without a sound escaping:
He shuddered at the straining of their throats.
And suddenly he watched them with suspicion.
Wondering if they were talking of his faults,
Were pitying him or seeing him with scorn.
He dived into their eyes and dragged up sneers,
And sauntering the streets, imagined laughter behind
him.
Working at odd jobs, ploughing, picking potatoes,
Chopping trees in the lumber woods in winter,
He became accustomed to an aimless and lonely labour.
He was solitary and unloquacious as a stone.
And silence grew over him like moss on an old stump.
But sometimes, going to town,
He was sore with the hunger for company among the people
And, getting drunk, would shout at them for friendship,
Laughing aloud in the streets.
He returned to the woods,
And dreaming at night of a shining cowboy heaven
Where guns crashed through his deafness, awoke morose,
And chopped the necks of pine trees in his anger.

The Bells in Silence

B.A. Bell
Ursuline College
Chatham, Ontario

Profound silence—
Before the great bells begin to ring,
Before the clappers begin to swing,
Before the bells begin to sing—
The bells, the bells, the bells!

Gentle swinging—
As the giant bells prepare to bong,
And the crashing notes - won't be too long
Before the bells begin their song—
And now, and now, and now!

Booming crashes—
As the clappers crash upon the lip,
As though dancing-the bells sway and dip,
The notes throughout my body rip—
But wait, but wait, but wait!

Profound silence—
As the huge bells continue ringing,
As the clappers continue crashing,
As the truth continues crying—
I'm deaf, I'm deaf, I'm deaf!

The Last Trip to Tulsa

Neil Young
Neil Young, Reprise RS 6317.
Copyright 1968 Cotillion Music Inc. & Broken Arrow Music,
1841 Broadway, N.Y., N.Y., 10023.

well i used to drive a cab, you know, heard a siren scream
pulled over to the corner and fell into a dream
there were two men eating pennies and three young girls who cried
"the west coast is falling, i see rocks in the sky"
the preacher took his bible and he laid it on the stool
he said, "with the congregation running, why should i play the fool?"

well, i used to be a woman, you know, i took you for a ride
i let you fly my airplane, it looked good for your pride
'cause you're the kind of man, you know, who likes what he says
i wonder what it's like to be so far over my head
well the lady made the wedding and she brought along the ring
she got down on her knees and said, "let's get on with this thing."

well i used to be a folk singer, keeping managers alive
when you saw me on a corner and told me i was jive
so i unlocked your mind, you know, to see what i could see
if you guarantee the postage, i'll mail you back the key
well i woke up in the morning with an arrow through my nose
there was an indian in the corner trying on my clothes.

well, i used to be asleep, you know, with blankets on my bed
i stayed there for a while 'til they discovered i was dead
the coroner was friendly and i liked him quite a lot
if i hadn't 've been a woman i guess i'd never have been caught
they gave me back my house and car and nothing more was said.

well i was driving down the freeway when my car ran out of gas
pulled over to the station but i was afraid to ask
the servicemen were yellow and the gasoline was green
although i knew i couldn't, i thought that i was gonna scream
that was on my last trip to tulsa just before the snow
if you ever need a ride there, be sure to let me know.

well i was chopping down a palm tree when a friend dropped by to ask
if i would feel less lonely if he helped me swing the axe
i said, "no, it's not a case of being lonely we have here
i've been working on this palm tree for eighty-seven years"
he said "go get lost" and walked toward his cadillac
i chopped down the palm tree and it landed on his back.

The Antlered Boy

Lloyd Abbey

I was different from other babies.

I poked my horns at the doctor
and came leaping out like a man from Mars,
firing a little beep-gun around the delivery room.

You should have seen the surprise on his face
when he opened the Cadillac womb:

plush bucket seats with ermine upholstery
and a little antenna to bring me
    the ball scores from Cleveland.

I don't know when he first caught on
that I came to possess my mother
but he's chased me out the hospital doors
with his army of orderlies after me

and I'm making a break down the highway
with the diesel ambulance hot on my tail—
Blood drips onto the pavement
from my trailing cord

They're on top of me!

I topple the roadside fruitstands down
    like double-decker buses
and bugger up the twelve-lane intersection.

Lying here by the traffic lights
with the Austin exhaling over my head
and the dog posing on top of me
awaiting my father's will

I can hear the thunder of Cadillacs
receding into the distance

while the strange trucks approach

loaded with antlers

The Execution

Alden Nowlan

On the night of the execution
a man at the door
mistook me for the coroner.
"Press," I said.

But he didn't understand. He led me
into the wrong room
where the sheriff greeted me:
"You're late, Padre."

"You're wrong," I told him. "I'm Press."
"Yes, of course, Reverend Press."
We went down a stairway.

"Ah, Mr. Ellis," said the deputy.
"Press!" I shouted. But he shoved me
through a black curtain.
The lights were so bright
I couldn't see the faces
of the men sitting
opposite. But, thank God, I thought
they can see me!

"Look!" I cried. "Look at my face!
Doesn't anybody know me?"

Then a hood covered my head.
"Don't make it harder for us," the hangman whispered.

from The Collected Works of Billy the Kid

Michael Ondaatje

After shooting Gregory
this is what happened

I'd shot him well and careful
made it explode under his heart
so it wouldnt last long and
was about to walk away
when this chicken paddles out to him
and as he was falling hops on his neck
digs the beak into his throat
straightens legs and heaves
a red and blue vein out

Meanwhile he fell
and the chicken walked away

still tugging at the vein
till it was 12 yards long
as if it held that body like a kite
Gregory's last words being

get away from me yer stupid chicken

Leonard Cohen

14

Earlier we spoke of the sense of space in Canadian poetry. In the work of Leonard Cohen, perhaps the greatest song-poet of them all, that sense becomes an exalting agony. As he knows full well, only a saint can cross the distances he perceives, and so his work becomes a continuous struggle for moments of sainthood. But as he says, even a saint is only "an escaped ski" whose "course is a caress of the hill". A saint for Cohen does not "dissolve the chaos, even for himself, for there is something arrogant and warlike in the notion of a man setting the universe in order. It is a kind of balance that is his glory."*

The "Story of Isaac", "Stories of the Street", and his prose-poem "God is Alive" illuminate these ideals. They also reveal Cohen's deep distrust of man's tendency to encase life in easy answers and manageable forms. Hovering between scepticism and faith, Cohen does not think that his dilemmas are merely personal. Paradoxically, he believes that our first step toward salvation is a heightened awareness of the terrible questions he asks. We must rediscover the crucifixion, says Cohen, "as a universal symbol" for "that's where man is at. On the cross."*

The first song, "Hey, That's No Way to Say Goodbye", seems to have nothing to do with these issues. But the careful listener will hear how the distances between man and woman that Cohen sings about in his love songs, lead naturally to his concern for the distances between humanity and God. The progression is most clearly expressed in Cohen's famous song, "Suzanne".**

*As quoted by William Kloman in a *New York Times* interview reprinted in *Songs of Leonard Cohen* (New York: Stranger Music, 1969), pp. 4-5.

**A grouping of poems that provides a partial interpretation of "Suzanne" may be found in Homer Hogan, *Poetry of Relevance*, (Agincourt, Ontario: Methuen, 1970), Vol. 2, pp. 170-175.

Hey, That's No Way
to Say Goodbye

Leonard Cohen
Songs of Leonard Cohen, Columbia CS9533.
Copyright 1967 Stranger Music Inc. Used by permission.

I loved you in the morning
Our kisses deep and warm
Your hair upon the pillow
Like a sleepy golden storm
Yes many loved before us
I know that we are not new
In city and in forest
They smiled like me and you
But now it's come to distances
And both of us must try
Your eyes are soft with sorrow
Hey, that's no way to say goodbye.

I'm not looking for another
As I wander in my time
Walk me to the corner
Our steps will always rhyme,
You know my love goes with you
As your love stays with me,
It's just the way it changes
Like the shoreline and the sea,
But let's not talk of love or chains
And things we can't untie,
Your eyes are soft with sorrow
Hey, that's no way to say goodbye.

I loved you in the morning
Our kisses deep and warm
Your hair upon the pillow
Like a sleepy golden storm
Yes, many loved before us
I know that we are not new
In city and in forest
They smiled like me and you
But let's not talk of love or chains
And things we can't untie,
Your eyes are soft with sorrow
Hey, that's no way to say goodbye.

For Maria*

Gérald Godin
translated by A.J.M. Smith and John Glassco

There's a plaster star on the ceiling of our white room
'when I die I want the smell of whisky all over the place
and I wanna sit on the knees of the finest female-angel of them all'
I'm longing for french speak french to me maria
in central park an old man with white hair
is he dreaming like me maria as I'll dream of you in a thousand years
of a girl he loved once
maria
I'll drop the anchor of my lips in you
forever drunk forever motionless   my arms like roots
rusty anchor of my ancient loves
I'll haul it up when my dead and gutted sea needs nothing
but the cold lightnings of the absent sun maria
my arms remembering better than I do the ragged beach
and the new ship that I was and come a long way
like a cry out of the storm and the rubble of wind
remembering the surf of love breaking
on the joint of the cross that we are   we'll go on forever joined!
maria
my girl of the breastlets
breastlets maria that's the breasts of a young girl
yes it's a new word I was the one who found it
it was in your blouse
maria my starched
bride

* Gérald Godin
does not consider
himself a Cana-
dian poet but
rather a "Québécois
poet. He agrees
to appear in this
Canadian anthology
solely in order
to have the oppor-
tunity to make
this fundamental
difference known.

spindle of my marvellous days
o one and only spindle   crossroads
of our four wishes
my dread voyage
my night my heart
o my mythology
maria my sweet my dark one
o my lies
o the keys to my dreams   my church of grey images
my far-off island my locust-tree my package tour
maria in the dark night
maria my composite bride
made up of all my loves
draw the curtain over our hearts
my finger walks on your arm   you take my hand
a spatter of spent desire runs through our veins
maria my soul I'll forget you my dark one
you'll draw the curtain over your memory
leaving me at the door   I'll forget you
as I take these clouds my memories by the neck
in their inverted image
before I drown in them
no one will see maria no one will see anything till the end of time
except my laughter glinting in the sun
but the words untied in my throat
the words maria
even spoken without me the words will call you

Story of Isaac

Leonard Cohen, **Songs from a Room**, Columbia CS 9767.

The door it opened slowly
And my father he came in
I was nine years old
And he stood so tall above me
His blue eyes they were shining
And his voice was very cold.
He said I've had a vision
And you know I'm strong and holy
I must do what I've been told.
So he started up the mountain
I was running, he was walking
And his axe was made of gold.

Well the trees they got much smaller
The lake a lady's mirror
We stopped to drink some wine
Then he threw the bottle over
It broke a minute later
And he put his hand on mine
I thought I saw an eagle
But it might have been a vulture
I never could decide
Then my father built an altar
He looked once behind his shoulder
He knew I would not hide.

You who build the altars now
To sacrifice these children
You must not do it any more
A scheme is not a vision
And you never have been tempted
By a demon or a God
You who stand above them now
Your hatchets blunt and bloody
You were not there before
When I lay upon a mountain
And my father's hand was trembling
With the beauty of the word.

And if you call me brother now
Forgive me if I inquire
Just according to whose plan
When it all comes down to dust
I will kill you if I must
I will help you if I can
When it all comes down to dust
I will help you if I must
I will kill you if I can
And mercy on our uniform
Man of peace, or
Man of war,
The peacock spreads his fan.

Belfast, 1971
(For John Benson, 1885-1971)

Eugene Benson

City of the 'saved'
On the banks of the Lagan
Below the aged and ageless hills;
City of my father
Eighty six years young
And dying
In this city of the damned.

His son, tanned and strong,
Forty three years young
(Off a high jet
Out of Toronto and Montreal
On the banks of the bright St. Lawrence),
Enters the father's room
Seeks out the father's hand.
Feather-limp the hand
And dying
In a city of the damned.

Outside the father's room,
A glasspane away,
The armoured cars
The guns
The rubber bullets
The steel bullets
The gas
The English soldiers tight with fear
In combat gear;
Inside the father's room,
A glasspane away,
The oxygen cylinder

The mask
The poisons, sad anodynes:
The father dying
In this city of the damned.

Heart gone, lungs ravished,
The flesh scourged to scarce a hundred pounds—
"My exact weight when I was ten years young"—
But the brain watching
The brain watching
Watching for the end.
The great root dying
In that city of the damned.

Heart gone
Lungs ravished
Ears that cannot hear;
Sphincter breaking
Tendons breaking
Chaos lurches near.
O father,
Hold these hands
Tanned and strong
Forty three years young;
O father dying
In a city of the damned.

Spare me the metal cylinder
And the gas and the mask
And the gunmen in the night;
Oh! Spare the father dying
In some city of the damned.

Stories of the Street

Leonard Cohen
Songs of Leonard Cohen, Columbia CS 9533.
Copyright 1967, 1969 Stranger Music Inc.
Used by permission. All rights reserved.

The stories of the street are mine
The Spanish voices laugh
The Cadillacs go creeping down
Through the night and the poison gas
And I lean from my window sill
In this old hotel I chose
Yes, one hand on my suicide
One hand on the rose.

I know you've heard it's over now
And war must surely come
The cities they are broke in half
And the middle men are gone
But let me ask you one more time
O, children of the dust,
All these hunters who are shrieking now
Do they speak for us?

And where do all these highways go
Now that we are free?
Why are the armies marching still
That were coming home to me?
O, lady with your legs so fine
O, stranger at your wheel
You are locked into your suffering
And your pleasures are the seal.

The age of lust is giving birth
And both the parents ask
The nurse to tell them fairy tales
On both sides of the glass
Now the infant with his cord
Is hauled in like a kite
And one eye filled with blueprints
One eye filled with night.

O, come with me my little one
And we will find that farm
And grow us grass and apples there
And keep all the animals warm
And if by chance I wake at night
And I ask you who I am
O, take me to the slaughter house
I will wait there with the lamb.

With one hand on a hexagram
And one hand on a girl
I balance on a wishing well
That all men call the world
We are so small between the stars
So large against the sky
And lost among the subway crowds
I try to catch your eye.

147

O Recruiting Sergeants!

Alfred Purdy

No, I'll not go with you to fight for
human freedom or power steering or
the sanctity of marriage in
Madrid and Troy and Detroit,
or join the freedom riders
on their gallant adventure
thru alabama and georgia—
I'm much too much
a bungling little mechanic and
dare not tinker among
the blind engineers of the universe
who work such cruelty and sorrow with
levers extending all the way down here,
and whose complaint dept. has
a dead switchboard—
    But to all you with burning barns,
lost causes and dishonoured flags,
washable skins and souls convulsed with
gallantry I say:
                Press on!

Mine is the cynicism no flag shall squander
(tho the ugly pregnant servant girl
in her last miscarried tormented ten minutes
((in the last reel or act or chapter))
turns out to have been my sister),
no lost cause claim casually
for its glorious dead;
no writhing murdered Christ
or bloody openmouthed Caesar
talked to death on the livingroom floor
inspires my soul to sob for any leader,
least of all yours—
Mine is the commonplace acceptance of good
or evil
        (a Persian at Marathon,
         a Turk at Lepanto),
the cynicism of
                the defeated majority that
wickedly survives
              virtue—

Xmas Eve 1971, Zihuatanejo

Irving Layton

Where were the men and where were the women robed in black
Where were the priests and nuns and the solemn processions
Now lights tear the jungle darkness, jukeboxes blare out their songs:
Packed in the open air cinema are all the reverent ones.

And only the lovely credulous children are in church
To hurrah His brithday and the marvelous manger story
Arrayed upon the altar; perhaps two or three old women
Crossing themselves in corners, remembering the Babe's past glory.

The children's eyes glisten as do those of the candy-stuffed
Animals that hang from ceiling and lone and radiant star
But absent are prayer and song, the breathtaking enchantment:
For service a boy in frayed jeans casually sweeps the floor.

O sanguine fairytale, here replayed among piñatas
Long-beaked hungering birds, white hotels, the pullulating poor;
I too rejoice at the glad tidings: now none shall be maimed or killed
For this sweet handsome doll saves no one. Come, let us adore.

Passover

Ken Guyatt
Westdale Secondary School
Hamilton, Ontario

We huddled together in our shelters
That stank of newly-slaughtered lamb,
That sticky night that would win our freedom,
That night when the moaning of the little ones hung like a
    siren on the fat air.
Little men in fallout shelters, we were,
Awaiting a holocaust.

We wondered what she looked like—that benevolent angel:
Like some dazzling goddess, we hoped,
Who dances on the stars
And sings of freedom with the voice of the untamed winds.
But the image of the smirking witch we had glimpsed so many times
On the horrid faces of our expiring elders
Could not be put aside.
And then each mind silently wondered
How our just God,
Our merciful God,
Could see fit to play the Hitler,
And we, the guilty beneficiaries.
And every heart fearfully asked
Why He would choose such an odd symbol
As a lamb's blood on the doorpost.

And once out on the desert,
With the sage at our head,
And the gently rippling waters behind,
We watched the sun sear the sky,
And listened to the still insistent cries of our bellies;
And our eyes were taunted by the laughing, dancing characters on
      the crumbling slabs of stone,
And our ears were pursued by the gurgling cries from some fishy
      kingdom.
So we huddled together on the desert sands,
Like pharaoh's entourage in some gilded tomb,
Vaguely stinking.
And every pair of anxious eyes
Groped.
And every pair of trembling lips
Murmured
Over and over again so as to make it more certain:
"Now, we are free."

Dance

Ann Farmer
Brockville Collegiate Institute
Brockville, Ontario

And all our paths have led us to
   the circle
   and joining hands we dance
   blood-dripped and wild
Screaming for a saviour
And tasting only pain
   for all our exhibition.

The Congregation

Marsha Searle
Glovertown Regional High School
Terra Nova, Newfoundland

You stumble into church
with your bible in your hand,
hear the word of God, and say—
"where is that man".
You say his name but you can't
say it plain,
and you wonder if you should say it at all.
You look across the aisle
and see that one-eyed midget, and say
"damn that man with his eye open".

A Story

Margaret Avison

Where *were* you then?
   At the beach.
With your crowd again.
Trailing around, open
to whatever's going. Which one's
calling for you tonight?
   Nobody.
I'm sorry I talk so. Young
is young. I ought to remember
and let you go and be glad.
   No. It's all right.
   I'd just sooner stay home.
You're not sick? did you
get too much sun? a crowd,
I never have liked it, safety in numbers
indeed!
   —He was alone.
Who was alone?
   The one
   out on the water, telling
   something. He sat in the boat that
   they shoved out for him, and told
   us things. We all just stood there
   about an hour. Nobody
   shoving. I couldn't see
   very clearly, but I listened
   the same as the rest.

What was it about?
      About a giant, sort of.
      No. No baby-book giant.
      But about a man. I think—
You *are* all right?
      Of course.
Then tell me
so I can follow. You all
standing there, getting up
out of the beach-towels and gathering
out of the cars, and the ones
half-dressed, not even caring—
      Yes. Because the ones
      who started to crowd around were
      so still. You couldn't
      help wondering. And it spread.
      And then when I would have felt out of it
      he got the boat, and I could
      see the white, a little, and
      hear him, word by word.
What did he tell the lot of you
to make you stand? Politics?
Preaching? You can't believe everything
they tell you, remember—
      No. More, well, a
      fable. Honestly, I—
I won't keep interrupting.
I'd really like you to tell.

Tell me. I won't say anything.
      It is a story. But
      only one man comes.
      Tall, sunburnt, coming
      not hurried, but as though
      there was so much power in reserve
      that walking all day and night
      would be lovlier than sleeping if
      sleeping meant missing it, easy
      and alive, and out there.
Where was it?
      On a kind of clamshell back.
      I mean country, like round about here,
      but his tallness, as he walked there
      made green and rock-gray and brown
      his floorway. And sky a brightness.
What was he doing? Just walking?
      No. Now it sounds strange
      but it wasn't, to hear.
      He was casting seed,
      only everywhere.
      On the roadway, out
      on the baldest stone,
      on the tussocky waste
      and in pockets of loam.

Seed? A farmer?
      A gardener rather
      but there was nothing
      like garden, mother.
      Only the queer
      dark way he went
      and the star-shine of
      the seed he spent.
(Seed you could see that way—)
      In showers. His fingers
      shed, like the gold
      of blowing autumnal
      woods in the wild.
      He carried no wallet
      or pouch or sack,
      but clouds of birds followed
      to buffet and peck
      on the road. And the rock
      sprouted new blades
      and thistle and stalk
      matted in, and the birds
      ran threading the tall grasses
      lush and fine
      in the pockets of deep earth—

You mean, in time
he left, and you saw
this happen?
      The hollow
      air scalded with sun.
      The first blades went sallow
      and dried, and the one
      who had walked, had only
      the choked-weed patches
      and a few thin files
      of windily, sunnily
      searching thirsty ones
      for his garden
      in all that place.
      But they flowered, and shed
      their strange heart's force
      in that wondering wilderness—
Where is he now?
      The gardener?
No. The storyteller
out on the water?
      He is alone.

      Perhaps a few
      who beached the boat and
      stayed, would know.

God is Alive
from Beautiful Losers

Leonard Cohen
Buffy Sainte-Marie, **Illuminations,** Vanguard BSD 79300.
Used by permission of McClelland and Stewart Limited.

. . . God is alive. Magic is afoot. God is alive. Magic is afoot. God is afoot. Magic
is alive. Alive is afoot. Magic never died. God never sickened. Many poor men lied.
Many sick men lied. Magic never weakened. Magic never hid. Magic always ruled.
God is afoot. God never died. God was ruler though his funeral lengthened. Though
his mourners thickened Magic never fled. Though his shrouds were hoisted the naked
God did live. Though his words were twisted the naked Magic thrived. Though his
death was published round and round the world the heart did not believe. Many
hurt men wondered. Many struck men bled. Magic never faltered. Magic always
led. Many stones were rolled but God would not lie down. Many wild men lied.
Many fat men listened. Though they offered stones Magic still was fed. Though
they locked their coffers God was always served. Magic is afoot. God rules. Alive
is afoot. Alive is in command. Many weak men hungered. Many strong men thrived.
Though they boasted solitude God was at their side. Nor the dreamer in his cell,
nor the captain on the hill. Magic is alive. Though his death was pardoned round and
round the world the heart would not believe. Though laws were carved in marble
they could not shelter men. Though altars built in parliaments they could not order
men. Police arrested Magic and Magic went with them for Magic loves the hungry.
But Magic would not tarry. It moves from arm to arm. It would not stay with them.
Magic is afoot. It cannot come to harm. It rests in an empty palm. It spawns in
an empty mind. But Magic is no instrument. Magic is the end. Many men drove
Magic but Magic stayed behind. Many strong men lied. They only passed through
Magic and out the other side. Many weak men lied. They came to God in secret
and though they left him nourished they would not tell who healed. Though mountains
danced before them they said that God was dead. Though his shrouds were hoisted
the naked God did live. This I mean to whisper to my mind. This I mean to laugh
with in my mind. This I mean my mind to serve till service is but Magic moving
through the world, and mind itself is Magic coursing through the flesh, and flesh
itself is Magic dancing on a clock, and time itself the Magic Length of God . . .

Biographical Index

Abbey, Lloyd, *The Antlered Boy,* p. 138
Born in London, Ontario, 1943. Student working
for Phil. M. at University of Toronto. His poetry
aims at "emotional intensity with formal control".
Poetry published in *Canada First,* Anansi, 1969.

*Abma, Sandra, *If You Can Tell me,* p. 77
Sandra Abma, age 14, is in grade 9 in Garson,
Ontario. She plans to attend university and then
to "go far up north to a cabin by a lake", where
she can "write and paint Nature".

Acorn, Milton, *Kiss,* p. 22; from *I Shout Love,*
p. 97; *I've Tasted My Blood,* p. 54
Born in Charlottetown, Prince Edward Island,
1923. Worked as a carpenter and began writing
poetry in the 1950's. Leading "revolutionary"
poet of Canada. Works: *In Love and Anger*
(1956), *Against a League of Liars* (1960), *The
Brains's the Target* (1960), *Jawbreakers* (1963),
58 poems by Milton Acorn (1963),
I've Tasted My Blood, a selected collection
edited by Al Purdy.

*Ahenakew, Barry, *Of Pride in Race—Written
in Anger,* p. 45
Born on the Mistawasis Reserve in Saskatchewan, Barry Ahenakew is 18, enrolled in grade 12
in Canwood, Saskatchewan. His future plans are
"somewhat undecided" because of "an identity
struggle" in which he is trying to preserve his
Indian way of life and at the same time succeed
in white society. He writes that "I originally
had plans of going to university where I could
study social psychology and later switch over to
law".

Anderson, Patrick, *Cold Colloquy,* p. 8
Born in England, 1915. Helped to found the "Pre-
view" group of Canadian poets—F.R. Scott, P.K.
Page included—in Montreal in 1942. Tried to com-
bine "the lyric and didactic" in social poetry.
Critic. Works: *A Tent for April* (1945), *The
White Centre* (1947), *The Colour as Naked*
(1953), *Snake Wine* (1955), *Search Me* (1957),
First Steps in Greece (1959), *The Character
Ball* (1963), *Smile of Apollo* (1964), *Dolphin
Days* (1963), *Across the Alps* (1969).

Atwood, Margaret, *Fragments: Beach,* p. 32;
The Lifeless Wife, p. 57; *Backdrop addresses
cowboy,* p. 114; *Eden is a Zoo,* p. 86
Born in Ottawa, 1939. University teacher, full-
time writer, a director of House of Anansi. Her
poetry explores barriers between man and being.
Poetry: *The Circle Game* (1966, Governor General's Award), *The Animals in That Country*
(1968, first prize in Centennial Commission
Competition), *The Journals of Susanna
Moodie* (1970), *Procedures For Underground*
(1970), *Power Politics* (1971). Novel: *The
Edible Woman* (1969) is being made into a film.

Avison, Margaret, *A Story,* p. 153
Born in Galt, Ontario in 1918. Librarian, English
teacher, now a social worker in a Toronto mission. Fuses people and religious sensibility. Works:
Winter Sun (1960), *The Dumbfounding* (1966).

Belford, Ken, *There's No Room,* p. 132
Born in 1946. Hunts and farms in South Hazleton,
British Columbia. Work: *Fireweed.*

*Bell, B.A. *The Bells in Silence,* p. 135
Betty Ann Bell is 17, enrolled in grade 10 near
Chatham, Ontario. She plans to study archeology
and Egyptology and to continue writing poetry.
Miss Bell is almost totally deaf.

Benson, Eugene, *Belfast 1971,* p. 146
Born in Belfast, 1928. Migrated to Canada, where
he is now teaching English at the University of
Guelph. He has written many plays which have
been performed on stage and radio, as well as
the libretto for an opera, *Heloise and Abelard,* to
be performed by the Canadian Opera Company in
1973. Methuen Publications will publish his anthology of Canadian Drama in 1973.

Birney, Earle, *Transcontinental,* p. 11; *Bill-
boards Build Freedom of Choice,* p. 115
Born in Calgary, 1904. Raised in the West.
Worked with the radical Left in New York.
Taught at the University of Toronto, University of
British Columbia. Poet-in-residence at various
universities, world traveller, and lecturer. Poetry:
David and Other Poems (1942), *Now is Time*
(1945, Governor General's Award). Many vol-
umes followed. Recent, *Rag and Bone Shop*
(1970). Novels: *Turvey* (1949) and *Down the
Long Table* (1955).

bissett, bill, *The Canadian,* p. 12; *ode to
frank silvera,* p. 37
Born in Halifax, Nova Scotia, 1939. Full-time
wanderer in Vancouver area. Artist, pioneer in
concrete and sound poetry. Edits *blewointment-
press.* Poetry: *nobody owns th earth,* 1971.
Record: *Awake in the red desert!*

Brewster, Elizabeth, *Jamie,* p. 134
Born in Chipman, New Brunswick, 1922. Libra-
rian, professor of English at the University of
Alberta from 1970. Critic. Works: *East Coast*
(1951), *Lillooet* (1954), *Roads and Other
Poems* (1957), *Passage of Summer* (1969).

*Burke, Pat, *Pride,* p. 45
A Métis living in the Northwest Territories, Pat

Burke is 21 and attends grade 12 in Fort Smith, North West Territories. He plans to take an Associate Diploma in Physical Education from Mount Royal College in Calgary, Alberta.

*Byrne, Judy, *Message from the Beholder,* p. 94
Judy Byrne is 17, enrolled in grade 13 in Belle River, Ontario. She plans to study journalism on a part-time basis while working for an airline.

*Cardinal, Garry, *Dialogue,* p. 22
A Canadian Indian, Garry Cardinal is 19, enrolled in grade 12 in Sherwood Park, Alberta. His school has recently published a collection of his poems entitled "Here Lies Charles Fredrik". After graduating, he plans a career in electronics engineering.

Chamberland, Paul, *Legend of the Morning,* p. 26
Born in Quebec, 1939. Leading Québecois poet, his work ranges from tender lyricism to calls for social justice and the independence of his country. Works: *Le Pays* (1963), *L'inavouable,* (1968), *L'afficheur hurlé* (1965), *Terre Québec* (1964), and *Gensès* (1962).

Cohen, Leonard, *Hey, That's No Way to Say Goodbye,* p. 142; *Story of Isaac,* p. 145; *Stories of the Street,* p. 147; *God is Alive,* p. 156
Born in Montreal, 1934 of a wealthy Westmount family. Dropped out of university graduate studies in Columbia. Full-time writer, shuttling between North America and the Greek island of Hydra. Now a singer-composer. Albums by Columbia: *Leonard Cohen, Songs from a Room, Songs of Love and Hate.* Poetry: *Let us Compare Mythologies* (1956), *Spice Box of Earth* (1961), *Flowers for Hitler* (1964), *Parasites of Heaven* (1966). Refused Governor General's award for *Selected Poems* (1968).

*Cuff, Jeffrey, *The House of the Old Woman,* p. 112
Born and raised in Newfoundland, Jeffrey A. Cuff is 16, enrolled in grade 11 in St. John's Newfoundland. He wants to study everything from chemistry to fine art and then perhaps to teach "in small seaside colleges of Newfoundland and England". Meanwhile he does not want to commit himself "to any one field of art or science".

*Dolen, Louise, *Poem,* p. 73
Louise Dolen, is 14. She is enrolled in grade 9 in Cochrane, Alberta, and hopes one day to become an airline stewardess.

Dumont, Jim, *For Joe MacKinaw,* p. 47
Jim Dumont is an active worker in the Canadian Indian movement. His poem, "For Joe MacKinaw" is not, he says, "really mine—only a poetic version of prophecy that has been handed down for generations" among his people.

*Ellis, Pat, *For P.H.E.,* p. 59
A native of British Columbia, Pat Ellis is 18 and enrolled in grade 12 in Mission City, British Columbia. Pat wants to travel, "especially in Canada". In the poet's own words, "God put me here—I'll leave it to Him to figure out what's going to happen."

*Farmer, Ann, *Dance,* p. 153
Ann Elizabeth Farmer is 18. She is enrolled in grade 12 in Brockville, Ontario. She hopes to study medicine at the University of Western Ontario.

Fetherling, Doug, *There's this old vaudeville skit . . .,* p. 125
Born in the United States, he's made Canada his home for the past several years. In his early twenties, he works as free-lance writer, critic, and broadcaster for CBC. Edits underground newspaper *Tabloid.* Poetry: *United States of Heaven* (1900), *Our Man in Utopia* (1971). Anthology: *Thumbprints* (1970).

*Fillmore, Joanne, *Life is so Strange,* p. 55
Born in Nova Scotia, 1953. Raised in several foster homes. Her poem, "Life is so Strange", is her first attempt, "written within twenty minutes after midnight". She is now enrolled in the Nova Scotia Teachers College, Truro, N.S.

*Frank, Sylvia, *Guy,* p. 17
Sylvia Frank is 17, enrolled in grade 13 in London, Ontario. She hopes to study photography and then do creative work in which she can integrate poems with photographs.

Gemmel, Poppy, *they sit confident,* p. 89
Born in Toronto, 1941. After completing school she became a musician, and as a singer has travelled around the world. In her own words, she "writes poetry in spasms". Her poetry has appeared in the magazine *Quarry.*

George, Chief Dan, *Lament for Confederation,* p. 46
Born in the Burrard Reserve No. 3, British Columbia, 1899. Chief of the Coast Salish Indian tribe for 12 years and named honourary Chief of the Shuswap and Squamish tribes. Famed for his acting in *Little Big Man,* Chief Dan George is a leading spokesman for all North American Indians. In 1971, he received the annual Human Relations Award of the Canadian Council of Christians and Jews. His "Lament for Confederation" was delivered before a crowd of 32,000 at Vancouver's Empire Stadium on July 1, 1967.

Godin, Gérald, *For Maria,* p. 143
Born in Quebec, 1938. Major Québecois poet. Refusing to consider himself in any way a Canadian poet, Godin has worked actively for Quebec

independence, and though he strongly opposes violence, he was arrested and detained in prison during the October Crisis. He has worked for Radio Canada and the National Film Board. In 1969, he joined the *Québec-Presse*. Works: *Les Cantouques* (1967), *Nouveaux Poèmes* (1963), *Poèmes et cantos* (1962), *Chansons très naïves* (1961).

Gotlieb, Phyllis, *In Season,* p. 83; *Pop! Goes the Easel,* p. 127
Born in Toronto, 1926. Lives in Toronto with husband and children. Poetry: *Within the Zodiac* (1964), *Ordinary, Moving* (1969). Novels: *Sunburst* (1964), *Why Should I House All the Grief?* (1969).

*Guyatt, Ken, *Passover,* p. 151
Enrolled in grade 12 in Hamilton, Ken Guyatt is 17. Future plans? "Intermittent life" is his reply.

*Hagerty, Margaret, *Chosen Fate,* p. 14
Margaret Hagerty is 17, enrolled in grade 12 in Thessalon, Ontario. After graduating, she intends to study journalism.

Hénault, Gilles, *The Prodigal Son,* p. 58
Born in Saint-Majorique, Quebec, 1920. Major Québecois poet. Worked as a journalist and Director of the Museum of Contemporary Art. Works: *Théâtre en plein air* (1946), *Totems* (1953), *Voyage au pays de mémoire* (1959), and *Sémaphore* (1962).

*Holtby, Stuart, *Touchstone,* p. 73
Stuart Holtby is 17, enrolled in grade 13 in Ottawa. He plans to study medicine at the University of Western Ontario and to continue writing poetry.

*Kahn, Rochelle, *Maniac,* p. 34
Rochelle Kahn, age 16, is enrolled in grade 12 in Oshawa, Ontario. She has no definite plans, but she would like to study humanities at university and "travel extensively from across Canada to the moon".

Klein, A.M. *Elijah,* p. 70
Born in Montreal, 1909. Practises law in Montreal. Poetry is deeply Jewish in feeling and conviction. Also tries to fuse English and French culture in poems about French Canada. Poetry: *Hath Not a Jew* (1940), *Hitleriad* (1944), *Poems* (1944), *The Rocking Chair and Other Poems* (1948). Novel: *The Second Scroll* (1951).

Lampman, Archibald, *Freedom,* p. 51
Born at Morpeth, Ontario, 1861. Died in 1899. Civil Service in Ottawa. A camping enthusiast. Works: *Among the Millet* (1888), *Lyrics of Earth* (1893). Collected edition, 1900.

Lane, Pat, *The Black Colt,* p. 79
Neil Patrick Lane was born in Nelson, British Columbia, in 1939. Works: *Letters from the Savage Mind* (1966, dedicated to Red Lane), *Separa-*

tions (1969), *Mountain Oysters* (1971), and the poster poems *For Rita—in Asylum* and *Calgary City Jail* (1969).

Lane, Red, *Marchlands V,* p. 20
Richard Stanley "Red" Lane was born in Nelson, British Columbia, 1936. A remarkably gifted poet, Red Lane died of a cerebral hemorrhage when he was 29. Works: *1962 Poems of Red Lane, Collected Poems,* ed. by Patrick and Elaine May Lane (1968), *War Cry* (1969). Seymour Mayne is planning a complete edition of Red Lane's works for release in 1973.

Lapointe, Gatien, *Your Country,* p. 17
Born in Sainte-Justine, Quebec, 1931. Teaches literature at the University of Montreal and is known as a "symbolist poet". Works: *Jour malaise* (1953), *Otages de le joie* (1955), *Le temps premier* (1962), for which he won the Prix du Club des Poètes de Paris, *Ode du Saint-Laurent précédée de j'appartiens de la terre* (1963, Governor General's Award).

Layton, Irving, *Keine Lazarovitch 1870-1959,* p. 85; *Xmas Eve 1971, Zihuatanejo,* p. 150
Born in Roumania, 1912. Moved to Montreal as a child. Made poetry a fighting issue in the forties —a leader of *First Statement, Preview, Northern Preview,* and *Contact Press.* Teaches English at York University. Poetry: *In the Midst of My Fever* (1954), *The Cold Green Element* (1955). Novels. *Here and Now* (1945), *A Red Carpet for the Sun* (1959, Governor General's Award). *Collected Poems* issued in 1972.

Leslie, Kenneth, *Sonnet from By Stubborn Stars,* p. 77
Born in Picton, N.S., 1892. Worked as a journalist and a democratic activist. Works: *Windward Rock* (1934), *Such a Din!* (1935), *Lowlands Low* (1936), *By Stubborn Stars* (1938, Governor General's Award), *The Poems of Kenneth Leslie* (1971).

Livesay, Dorothy, *The Metal and the Flower,* p. 121
Born in Winnipeg, 1909. Scholar, journalist, teacher, social worker, and a democratic activist. Works: *Green Pitcher* (1928), *Signpost* (1932), *Day and Night* (1944), *Poems for People* (1947, Governor General's Award).

*Longard, Cass, *Waterfront,* p. 63
Cass Longard is 16, enrolled in grade 11 in Halifax County, Nova Scotia. Future plans: "To travel and see everything there is to see and feel everything there is to feel".

MacEwen, Gwendolyn, *Manzini: Escape Artist,* p. 79; *Skulls and Drums,* p. 107; *Generation Cometh,* p. 121
Born in Toronto, 1941. At fifteen, wrote poetry for

Canadian Forum. Dropped out of school to be full-time writer. Concerned with myth and joy. Poetry: *Selah* (1960), *The Drunken Clock* (1961), *The Rising Fire* (1963), *A Breakfast for Barbarians* (1966), *The Shadow-Maker* (1969, Governor General's Award). Novels: *Julian the Magician* (1963), *The Twelve Circles of the Night.*

Mair, Charles, from *Tecumseh,* p. 6
Born in Lanark, Upper Canada, 1838. Died in 1927. Worked for federal government, built roads, captured by Louis Riel in 1869, explored British Columbia. Works: *Dreamland and Other Poems* (1868), *Tecumseh: A Drama* (1886), *Through the Mackenzie Basin* (1908). Collected works in 1926.

Mandel, Eli, *The Meaning of the I CHING,* p. 102; *"Marina",* p. 108
Born in Estevan, Saskatchewan, 1922. Professor in Fine Arts and Humanities at York University. Critic, editor. Works: *Fuseli Poems* (1960), *Black and Secret Man* (1969), *An Idiot Joy* (1967, Governor General's Award).

Miron, Gaston, *October,* p. 16
Born in Quebec, 1928. Award-winning poet and editor. Works: *Deux sangs* (1953), *L'homme rapaillé* (1970). He reads his poetry in *La Nuit de la Poésie,* an important film produced in 1971 by O.N.F., which presents many of the major Québecois poets.

*Murdoch, Liz, *Oh, Oh, Canada!,* p. 117
A native of Alberta, Miss Murdoch is enrolled in grade 11 in Calgary. Now 17, she plans a career in journalism or television "with a good deal of free time devoted to working with horses".

*Nagy, Eve, *Birdless Skies,* p. 73
Eve Nagy, age 15, is in grade 9 in Calgary, Alberta.

Nelligan, Emile, *Before Two Portraits of My Mother,* p. 86
Born in Montreal, 1879. Wrote brilliant poetry between 15 and 20 years of age, when insanity claimed him. For the next 42 years, he lived in mental institutions. He died in 1941. Collections of the poems which made him one of the greatest poets of Quebec include *Emile Nelligan et son oeuvre,* ed. Louis Dantin (1903), *Poésies complètes,* 1896-1899, ed. L. Lacourcière (1952), and *Emile Nelligan: Sources et originalité,* ed. Paul Wyczynski, 1960. An English translation of some of his works was made by P.F. Widdows in *Selected poems* (1960).

Nichol, bp. *The Natural Thing,* p. 28
Born in Vancouver, 1944. Studied for a year at the University of British Columbia. Works at the University of Toronto library, co-edits the poetry

magazine, *Ganglia.* One of the best-known of Canada's younger poets, he is especially noted for his experiments with typography and sound in composing poetry. Works: *Monotones* (1971), *The Other Side of the Moon* (1971), *The Aleph Beth Book* (1971), *Still Water* (1970), *The True Eventual Story of Billy the Kid* (1970), *Night on Prose Mountain* (1969), *Journeying and the Return* (1967).

Nowlan, Alden, *I, Icarus,* p. 29; *The Execution,* p.139
Born in Nova Scotia, 1933. Worked as farm labourer, sawmill worker, and a journalist with *Telegraph-Journal* of Saint John, New Brunswick. Maritime poetry, concerned with the plight of common man in Canadian culture. Poetry: *The Rose and the Puritan* (1958), *A Darkness in the Earth* (1959), *Wind in a Rocky Country* (1960), *Bread, Wine, and Salt* (1967, Governor General's Award). *Playing the Jesus Game* (1970). Drama and short stories: *Miracle at Indian River* (1968).

Ondaatje, Michael, from *The Collected Works of Billy the Kid,* p. 139
Born in Ceylon, 1943. Came to Canada in 1962. Teaches English at universities. Writes dramatic, bizarre poetry. Works: *The Dainty Monsters* (1967), *The Man With Seven Toes* (1969), *The Collected Works of Billy the Kid* (1970). Critical study: *Leonard Cohen* (1970). Film on bp Nichol to be called *Sons of Captain Poetry.*

*Paterson, Craig, *Nails,* p. 50
Craig Paterson is 17. He is enrolled in grade 12 and lives at Vedder Crossing, British Columbia. He plans to study musical composition at the University of B.C. and then "to get further involved in music and writing".

Plourde, Marc, *growing up: 1950's,* p. 110
Born in Montreal, 1951. French-Canadian and English-Canadian parents. Works published by Fiddlehead Poetry Books.

Pratt, E.J., *The Precambrian Shield,* p. 7
Born in Western Bay, Newfoundland, 1883. Died in 1964. Professor of English at University of Toronto. Noted for the almost epic quality of his narrative poems. One of his great poems is *Towards the Last Spike* (1952), on the building of the Canadian Pacific Railway. *Collected Poems* (1944). Second edition of *Collected Poems* in 1958.

Purdy, Al, *O Recruiting Sergeants,* p. 148
Born in Wooler, Ontario, 1918. Dropped out of school at 16. Odd jobs. Lives now in Ameliasburg, Ontario, from where he wanders. Anthologist. Works: *The Caribou Horses* (1965, Governor

General's Award), North of Summer (1967),
Poems for All the Annettes (1968), *Wild Grape
Vine* (1968), *Love in a Burning Building* (1970).
Reaney, James, *Klaxon,* p. 110
Born in Stratford, Ontario, 1926. Professor of
English at University of Western Ontario. Edits
the literary magazine, *Alphabet.* Works: *The
Red Heart* (1949 Governor General's Award),
A Suit of Nettles (1958), *Twelve Letters to a
Small Town* (1926), *The Killdeer and other
plays* (1962), *Colours in the Dark* (1970).
Scott, F.R., *Eden,* p. 120
Born in Quebec City, 1899. Professor of law at
McGill University. Major commentator on Cana-
dian political economy. Verse ranges from satire
to love poems. Fine translator. Works: *Overture*
(1945), *Events and Signals* (1954). More re-
cent works are *Selected Poems* and *Trou-
vailles.*
*Searle, Marsha, *The Congregation,* p. 153
Marsha Searle is 18. Living in the beautiful Terra
Nova National Park of Newfoundland, she is
enrolled in grade 11 and plans to be a "physical
education and recreation instructor with the
Canadian Armed Forces."
Service, Robert W., *The Spell of the Yukon,*
p. 64
Born in Lancashire, England, 1874. Died in 1958.
Worked at odd jobs in the West Coast, the Far
North and the Yukon District. Works: *Songs of a
Sourdough* (1907), *Bar-Room Ballads* (1940),
Complete Poems (1941).
Smith, A.J.M., *The Sorcerer,* p. 69
Born in Montreal, 1902. Professor of English,
critic, editor, translator, anthologist, and poet
Poetry: *News of the Phoenix* (1945, Governor
General's Award), *A Sort of Ecstasy: Poems
New and Selected* (1954), *Collected Poems*
(1962). A recent work is his study, *The Poetry
of P.K. Page* (1971).
Souster, Raymond, *Flight of the Roller-Coaster,*
p. 71
Born in Toronto, 1921. Banker in Toronto. Organ-
izer of *Contact Press.* Anthologist. Works:
When We Are Young (1946), *Go to Sleep, World*
(1947), *City Hall Street* (1952), *The Colour of
the Times* (1964, Governor General's Award),
So Far So Good (1969).
*Sterling, Mary Jane, *Thoughts on Silence,*
p. 41
A member of the Nteakyapamuk Indian tribe in
British Columbia, Mary Jane Sterling wrote this
poem while she was attending a residential school
on Vancouver Island.
*Straubergs, Maruta, *A Blatant Cancer,* p. 89

Enrolled in grade 12 in Calgary, Alberta, Maruta
Straubergs is 17 and plans to study psychology at
Simon Fraser University "in order to make a living while engaging in writing, my main interest".
Her greatest wish is "to remain human in the
midst of this machine-oriented society, and to
reach out to others who need humanity as much
as myself".
Stump, Sarain, *I Was Mixing Stars and Sand,*
p. 44
Born in Wyoming, 1945. Educated by his Indian
relatives from the Shoshone, Cree, and Flathead
(Salish) tribes who passed on to him the stories of
their heritages. Mr. Stump has settled in Eden
Valley, Alberta. In 1970, Gray's Publishing Co. in
Sidney, British Columbia, printed a remarkable
collection of "ethnic poem-drawings" by Sarain
Stump. Readers are urged to consult this book in
order to see how much force and meaning Stump's
poems receive from his etchings.
Trottier, Pierre, *State of Siege,* p. 93
Born in Montreal, 1925. Became a member of the
Department of External Affairs in 1947 and
served in embassies in Moscow, Djakarta, and
London. Works: *Le combat contre Tristan* (1951),
Poèmes de Russie (1957), *Les belles au bois
dormant* (1960), and *Mon Babel* (1963), a collection of essays.
Trower, Peter, *siddhartha in the south wing,*
p. 101
Born in St. Leonards, England, 1930. Emigrated
to Canada where he settled on the West Coast,
working as logger, surveyor, cartoonist, freelance
writer, poet, and songwriter. He is now becoming
increasingly recognized as a leading writer and
publisher of West Coast poetry. Works: *Poems
for a Dark Sunday* (1964), *Moving Through the
Mystery* (1969), *Between the Sky and the Splinters* (1972).
Waddington, Miriam, *Love poem,* p. 76
Born in Winnipeg, 1917. Social case worker. Lived
many years in Montreal. Critic, lectures now at
York University. Works: *Green World* (1945),
Second Silence (1955), *Season's Lovers* (1958),
Glass Trumpet (1966), *Say Yes* (1969), *Dream
Telescope* (1970), *Call Them Canadians* .(1968).
*Wendt, Frederik, *Conversation,* p. 37
A native of Nova Scotia, Frederik Wendt is 18,
enrolled in grade 12 near Ellershouse, N.S. He
plans to move to the West Coast and become a
carpenter.
Williams, Gordon, *The Last Crackle,* p. 42
A member of both the Okanagan and Shuswap
Indian tribes of British Columbia, Gordon Wil-
liams was born in Vernon, British Columbia and

163

hopes to continue writing poetry.

Yukich, Kenneth, *When I Was Eight,* p. 89; *Happy Birthday Kid,* p. 129

Born in Sault Sainte Marie, 1946. Left home at 17 and joined the navy for three years. Has recently been travelling in Canada. Poetry published in *T.O. Now, The Young Toronto Poets,* House of Anansi, 1968.

Zieroth, Dale, *Father,* p. 84

Born in Neepaw, Manitoba, 1946. Worked on parents' farm. Taught high school, worked in free school movement and as book shipper. Lives in Toronto. With wife, edits *Another poetry magazine.* Poems appeared in various anthologies and magazines, most recently in *Mindscapes,* House of Anansi, 1971.

Acknowledgements

The Antlered Boy by Lloyd Abbey. Reprinted from *Canada First: A Mare Usque Ad Edmonton: New Canadian Poets,* 1969, by permission of House of Anansi Press Limited.

Backdrop addresses cowboy by Margaret Atwood. Reprinted from *The Animals in That Country* by Margaret Atwood, by permission of Oxford University Press, Toronto.

Before Two Portraits of My Mother by Emile Nelligan, trans. George Johnston. Reprinted from *The Poetry of French Canada in Translation,* John Glassco, editor, by permission of the translator.

Belfast 1971 by Eugene Benson. Reprinted by permission of the author.

Billboards Build Freedom of Choice by Earle Birney. Reprinted from *Selected Poems 1966* by Earle Birney, by permission of The Canadian Publishers, McClelland and Stewart Limited, Toronto.

The Black Colt by Pat Lane. Reprinted from *Mountain Oysters,* by permission of the author.

The Canadian by bill bissett. Reprinted from *Made in Canada: New Poems of the Seventies,* by permission of Oberon Press.

Cold Colloquy by Patrick Anderson. Reprinted from "Poem on Canada" in *The White Centre* by Patrick Anderson, The Ryerson Press, by permission of McGraw-Hill Ryerson Limited.

from **The Collected Works of Billy the Kid** by Michael Ondaatje. Reprinted by permission of House of Anansi Press Limited.

Dead Man's Song Dreamed by One Who is Alive. Reprinted from *Beyond The High Hills: A Book of Eskimo Poems,* ed. Knud Rasmussen. © 1961 The World Publishing Company.

Eden by F.R Scott. Reprinted by permission of the author.

Eden is a Zoo by Margaret Atwood. Reprinted from *Procedures For Underground* by Margaret Atwood, by permission of Oxford University Press, Toronto.

Elijah by A.M. Klein. Reprinted from *Hath Not A Jew* by A.M. Klein, published by Behrman House, New York.

The Execution by Alden Nowlan. Reprinted by permission of the author.

Father by Dale Zieroth. Reprinted from *Soundings: New Canadian Poets,* 1970, by permission of House of Anansi Press Limited.

Flight of the Roller-Coaster by Raymond Souster. Reprinted from *The Colour of the Times* by Raymond Souster, Ryerson Press, by permission of McGraw-Hill Ryerson Limited.

for Joe MacKinaw by Jim Dumont. Reprinted from *TAWOW* by permission of the author.

For Maria by Gerald Godin, trans. A.J.M. Smith and John Glassco. Reprinted by permission of the author and the translators.

Fragments: Beach by Margaret Atwood. Reprinted from *Procedures For Underground* by Margaret Atwood, by permission of Oxford University Press, Toronto.

Generation Cometh by Gwendolyn MacEwen. Reprinted from *The Rising Fire* by Gwendolyn MacEwen, by permission of the author.

growing up: 1950's by Marc Plourde. Reprinted by permission of the author.

God Is Alive from *Beautiful Losers* by Leonard Cohen. Reprinted by permission of the Canadian Publishers, McClelland and Stewart Limited, Toronto.

Happy Birthday Kid by Kenneth Yukich. Reprinted from *The Young Toronto Poets,* 1968, by permission of House of Anansi Press Limited.

Hard Times. Reprinted from *Beyond the High Hills, A Book of Eskimo Poems,* edited by Knut Rasmussen. Copyright © 1961 by The World Publishing Company.

I, Icarus by Alden Nowlan. Reprinted from *Bread, Wine and Salt* by Alden Nowlan, © 1961 by Clarke, Irwin & Company Limited.

from **I Shout Love** by Milton Acorn. Reprinted courtesy of McGraw-Hill Ryerson.

I Was Mixing Stars and Sand by Sarain Stump. Reprinted from *There is My People Sleeping,* 1970, Gray's Publishing Ltd., Sidney, British Columbia, by permission.

In Season by Phyllis Gotlieb. Reprinted from *Ordinary, Moving* by Phyllis Gotlieb by permission of Oxford University Press, Toronto.

I've Tasted My Blood by Milton Acorn. Reprinted courtesy of McGraw-Hill Ryerson.

Jamie by Elizabeth Brewster. Reprinted from *Passage of Summer* by Elizabeth Brewster, The Ryerson Press, by permission of McGraw-Hill Ryerson Limited.

Keine Lazarovitch 1870-1959 by Irving Layton. Reprinted from *The Swinging Flesh* by Irving Layton, by permission of The Canadian Publishers, McClelland and Stewart Limited, Toronto.

Kiss by Milton Acorn. Reprinted courtesy of McGraw-Hill Ryerson.

Klaxon by James Reaney. Reprinted from *The Red Heart* by James Reaney, by permission of the author and his literary agent, Sybil Hutchinson.

A Lament for Confederation by Chief Dan George. Reprinted from *TAWOW.*

The Last Crackle by Gordon Williams. Reprinted from *I Am an Indian,* Dent & Sons (Canada) Limited.

Legend of the Morning by Paul Chamberland, trans. John Glassco. Reprinted by permission of the translator.

Life is so Strange by Joanne Fillmore. Reprinted by permission of the author.

The Lifeless Wife by Margaret Atwood. Reprinted by permission of the author.

Love poem by Miriam Waddington. Reprinted from *Say Yes* by Miriam Waddington, by permission of Oxford University Press, Toronto.

Manzini: Escape Artist by Gwendolyn MacEwen. Reprinted from *A Breakfast for Barbarians* by Gwendolyn MacEwen, The Ryerson Press, by permission of McGraw-Hill Ryerson Limited.

Marchlands V by Red Lane. Reprinted by permission from *Collected Poems of Red Lane,* eds. Patrick Lane and Seymour Mayne, Very Stone House, Vancouver, 1968.

Marina by Eli Mandel. Reprinted from *An Idiot Joy* by Eli Mandel, by permission of the author.

The Meaning of the I Ching by Eli Mandel. Reprinted from *An Idiot Joy* by Eli Mandel, by permission of the author.

The Metal and the Flower by Dorothy Livesay. Reprinted by permission of the author.
The Natural Thing by bp Nichol. Reprinted by permission of the author from *New Wave Canada: The New Explosion in Canadian Poetry* by bp Nichol.
O Recruiting Sergeants! by Alfred Purdy. Reprinted from *Poems for all the Annettes,* 1968, by permission of House of Anansi Press Limited.
October by Gaston Miron, trans. Fred Cogswell. Reprinted by permission of the translator.
ode to frank silvera by bill bissett. Reprinted from *nobody owns th earth,* 1971 by bill bissett, by permission of House of Anansi Press Limited.
Pop! Goes the Easel by Phyllis Gotlieb. Reprinted from *Ordinary, Moving,* by permission of Oxford University Press, Toronto.
The Precambrian Shield by E. J. Pratt. Reprinted by permission of The Macmillan Company of Canada Limited from the poem "Towards the Last Spike" in *Collected Poems* by E. J. Pratt.
The Prodigal Son by Gilles Hénault, trans. F. R. Scott. Reprinted from *The Poetry of French Canada in Translation,* by permission of the translator.
siddhartha in the south wing by Peter Trower. Originally from *Moving Through the Mystery,* Vancouver, Talonbooks, 1969. Reprinted in *West Coast Seen, An Anthology of West Coast Poetry,* eds. Jim Brown and David Phillips, Talonbooks, Vancouver, 1969.
Skulls and Drums by Gwendolyn MacEwen. Reprinted from *The Rising Fire* by Gwendolyn MacEwen, by permission of the author.
Song to the Wanderer by Hermia Harris Fraser. Reprinted from *Songs of the Western Islands,* by Hermia Harris Fraser, Ryerson Press, by permission of McGraw-Hill Ryerson Limited.
Sonnet by Kenneth Leslie. Reprinted from *By Stubborn Stars* by Kenneth Leslie, The Ryerson Press, by permission of McGraw-Hill Ryerson Limited.
The Sorcerer by A. J. M. Smith. Reprinted from *Collected Poems* by A. J. M. Smith, by permission of Oxford University Press, Toronto.
The Spell of the Yukon by Robert W. Service. Reprinted from *Collected Poems of Robert Service,* The Ryerson Press, by permission of McGraw-Hill Ryerson Limited.
State of Siege by Pierre Trottier, trans. F. R. Scott. Reprinted by permission of the translator.
A Story by Margaret Avison. Reprinted by permission of the author from *Modern Canadian Verse,* Oxford University Press, Toronto, 1967.
from **Tecumseh** by Charles Mair. Reprinted from *Tecumseh* by Charles Mair, The Ryerson Press, by permission of McGraw-Hill Ryerson Limited.
There's No Room by Ken Belford. Originally from *Fireweed,* Talonbooks, Vancouver, 1967. Reprinted in *West Coast Seen, An Anthology of West Coast Poetry,* eds. Jim Brown and David Phillips, Talonbooks, Vancouver, 1969.
There's this old vaudeville skit . . . by Doug Fetherling. Reprinted from *T. O. Now, The Young Toronto Poets,* 1968, by permission of House of Anansi Press Limited.
they sit confident by Poppy Gemmell. Reprinted by permission of the author.

Thoughts on Silence by Mary Jane Sterling. Reprinted from *I am an Indian,* Dent & Sons (Canada) Limited.
Transcontinental by Earle Birney from *Selected Poems,* 1966, by Earle Birney. Reprinted by permission of The Canadian Publishers, McLelland and Stewart Limited, Toronto.
Wabanaki Song trans. Mrs. Wallace Brown. Reprinted from *The Penguin Book of Canadian Verse,* ed. Ralph Gustafson, Penguin Books, 1958, by permission of the editor.
When I Was Eight by Kenneth Yukich. Reprinted from *T. O. Now, The Young Toronto Poets,* 1968, by permission of House of Anansi Press Limited.
Xmas Eve 1971, Zihuatanejo by Irving Layton. Reprinted by permission of the author.
Your Country by Gatien Lapointe, trans. John Glassco. Reprinted by permission of the translator.

And special thanks to the following high school student poets: Margaret Hagerty, Sylvia Frank, Garry Cardinal, Rochelle Kahn, Frederik Wendt, Pat Burke, Barry Ahenakew, Craig Paterson, Joanne Fillmore, Pat Ellis, Cass Longard, Louise Dolen, Stuart Holtby, Eve Nagy, Sandra Abma, Maruta Straubergs, Judy Byrne, Jeffrey Cuff, Liz Murdoch, Betty Ann Bell, Ken Quyatt, Ann Farmer, and Marsha Searle.

Note: The editor and publisher have made every reasonable effort to ensure that these acknowledgements are complete and correct. Apology is made for any inadvertent errors or omissions.